I0819473

100 HIKES OF A LIFETIME U.S.A.

100 HIKES OF A LIFETIME U.S.A.

The Country's Ultimate Scenic Trails

STEPHANIE PEARSON

WASHINGTON, D.C.

CONTENTS

LEFT: The Hoh River Trail in Washington State (page 118) offers a unique hike through rainforest scenery.

PAGES 2-3: Find epic views on a hike to the summit of Mount Mansfield in Vermont (page 244).

INTRODUCTION

One sultry September evening, my partner Brian and I set off at sunset to hike a section of North Dakota's Maah Daah Hey Trail (page 360). This 144-mile-long path is a portal into the Badlands, an exotic landscape at odds with the surrounding Great Plains. It traverses Theodore Roosevelt National Park and beyond, rising over pastel buttes and mesas and occasionally dead-ending at an intimidating herd of bison.

The trail switchbacked a few hundred feet up through a tight canyon with a narrow view of the darkening sky. As we turned a corner onto a west-facing ridgeline, the heavens broke loose with pyrotechnics so fierce that I wondered if Zeus himself had pegged us for target practice. We ran for lower ground, but not before I noticed the quote inscribed on a trail marker: "In every walk with Nature one receives far more than he seeks."

This phrase, written by John Muir in 1877, sums up my lifetime of hiking adventures. They began in northern Minnesota in the 1970s when my mom and dad took my four siblings and me on Sunday hikes along Lake Superior's North Shore. To my eight-year-old legs these adventures felt like Type 3 fun, a painful march through the autumn colors, even if they were only a few miles and most ended at a spectacular waterfall.

Those first forays awoke in my body a rhythm as old as humanity itself, an awareness that hiking—whether in solitary wilderness or at the edge of a city—is the best way to be at peace with the soul, a natural act to balance mental and physical well-being. I've been lucky to reach some exotic places by foot: Himalayan peaks, penguin colonies on the Falkland Islands (Islas Malvinas), and unpeopled Brazilian beaches to name a few. But I have lately come to realize that sometimes the best hikes are the ones that don't require a passport and are easily accessible out my back door.

KNOW BEFORE YOU GO

Always check National Park Service, state park, trail, and recreational websites before planning your trip for the latest updates on trail status and closures.

ABOVE: **Hikers may get lucky and spot a moose or two in Maine's Baxter State Park on the Mount Katahdin Loop (page 196).**

PAGES 8-9: **Come spring, North Carolina's Mountains-to-Sea Trail (page 296) blooms with Catawba rhododendrons along the Blue Ridge Parkway.**

My parents understood that. So did U.S. Secretary of the Interior Stewart Udall, who championed the National Trails System Act, signed by President Lyndon B. Johnson in 1968. "A national trail is a gateway into nature's secret beauties, a portal to the past, a way into solitude and community," Udall said. "It is also an inroad to our national character. Our trails are both irresistible and indispensable."

The National Trails System Act called for creating trails in both urban and rural settings accessible to people of all ages, interests, and physical abilities. It promoted the enjoyment and appreciation of trails while encouraging greater public access.

Today the National Trails System includes 88,600 miles of paths and consists of 11 national scenic trails, 19 national historic trails, and 1,300 national recreation trails. These paths wind through 70 wildlife refuges, 80 national parks, 90 national forests, 90 Bureau of Land Management areas,

123 wilderness areas, and 100 major metropolitan areas. Better yet, more than 230 million Americans live within 60 miles of a national trail.

This book celebrates these paths and includes icons like the Appalachian Trail (page 190) alongside less discovered jewels like Wisconsin's Ice Age National Scenic Trail (page 380). But not all the paths I chose to include are part of the National Trails System. One example is the *Wanderer* Memory Trail on Jekyll Island, Georgia (page 278). This half-mile interpretive path tells the story of the *Wanderer,* a ship that illegally trafficked 490 enslaved humans from Africa after the slave trade had been outlawed.

Other than hiking, the greatest joy in writing this book came from meeting people across the country who are deeply passionate about their own backyard trails. Some are federal, state, county, or municipal employees; others work for nonprofit organizations; and others are volunteers. Whether they raise funds, wield a chain saw, or clean privies, these people make it possible for the rest of us to meander in peace, despite increasing threats to the trails, which include damage from more powerful storms, enormous funding cuts, overuse, and neglect.

My hope is that this book will lead you to a few undiscovered paths that provide a mixture of joy, adventure, solitude, and beauty. I hope these trails inspire you to pay it forward so that they will live on into the future.

RULES OF THE TRAIL

Acquire the proper permits. The most popular trails require permits—some must be acquired months in advance, while others can be purchased the day of the hike.

Be prepared. Buy a good map and research the route—where to park, where to camp, and any potential dangers along the trail. (This book will come in handy!) Learn what wildlife you may encounter, the weather patterns, and what gear is necessary to safely undertake the hike. Invest in a compass or GPS and know how to use them.

Respect fellow hikers. Trails are for everyone. Be patient—not all hikers move at the same pace. Be polite, especially if passing a fellow hiker. Keep conversation to a minimum when other hikers are within earshot.

Leave no trace. Pack out what you pack in. If camping, leave the campsite free of trash and better than you found it.

Follow the rules. Rules are in place to protect the landscape, the wildlife living within it, and fellow hikers. Following the rules mitigates harm to all.

Steer clear. It may be tempting to take a close-up of charismatic flora and fauna to post on social media, but give wildlife space. That means generally the length of a football field for bears, bison, and other big mammals. Leave the rest of the environment—rocks, flowers, bird nests, and other potential natural keepsakes—where you found them.

Give back. Most trails exist because an army of volunteers maintain them. Donate time, money, or resources to the trails you love the most.

OPPOSITE: **There's nothing like the epic landscapes seen on Alaska's Harding Icefield Trail (page 132).**

PART ONE

THE WEST & THE PACIFIC

Wildflowers bloom along the Wonderland Trail (page 112), which wraps its way around majestic Mount Rainier in Washington State.

ARIZONA

NORTH KAIBAB TO BRIGHT ANGEL TRAIL

Rim to Rim in Grand Canyon National Park

DISTANCE: 24 miles one-way **LENGTH OF TRIP:** 1 to 4 days **BEST TIME TO GO:** Spring or fall **DIFFICULTY:** Strenuous

"Sublime," "perilous," and "spiritual" are just a few adjectives that describe hiking into the depths of a canyon that was formed roughly six million years ago by the forces of the Colorado River. Below the rim of the Grand Canyon is an alternate universe, one in which humans have roamed for 12,000 years through layers of exposed rock that date back as far as 1.8 billion years. Curtains of water cascade from impossible heights; cacti cling to rocks in miraculous ways; condors soar overhead.

Who wouldn't want to explore such an otherworldly place? Yet of the nearly five million annual visitors who pass through Grand Canyon National Park, less than one percent attempt this iconic rim-to-rim hike. Of those who complete it, almost all report that the hike is more difficult than expected.

There's good reason for that misperception. Hiking in the Grand Canyon is the inverse of mountain climbing: It starts with a descent and ends with a steep climb back up. There's also extreme desert terrain, very few water sources, and temperatures that regularly soar well past 100°F on the hottest summer days and fall far below freezing in the winter.

The perils are many, but the reward is an adventure like no other. Starting at the North Kaibab trailhead, which is at an elevation of 8,241 feet (more

KNOW BEFORE YOU GO

Hiking rim to rim requires a 220-mile, 4.5-hour drive around the canyon to return to your starting point. To skip the shuttle, train for the 48-mile rim-to-rim-to-rim hike, climbing back out to the North Kaibab trailhead.

OPPOSITE: Gaze down at the Colorado River from 3,000 feet above on the canyon's rim.

PAGES 16–17: End your rim-to-rim hike with the 4,400-foot climb up the Bright Angel Trail.

than 1,000 feet higher than any trailhead on the South Rim), hikers descend along the least visited and most difficult of the three major inner canyon trails. Along the way, they'll pass through nearly every ecosystem that exists between Canada and Mexico.

The North Kaibab also makes its way through Supai Tunnel, a hole in the Redwall Limestone that Park Service crews blasted through with dynamite in the 1920s, then meanders precipitously along a path carved out of the towering Redwall Limestone before descending to the flats of Bright Angel Canyon and Roaring Springs, where water cascades from the cliffs into Bright Angel Creek. Soon after is Cottonwood, the first of three designated campgrounds for hikers.

The 7.2-mile section between Cottonwood Campground and Phantom Ranch—the only lodge in the park below the canyon rim—is known as the Inner Gorge, a canyon with walls of 1.7-billion-year-old black Vishnu Schist that can bake hikers to a crisp on hot summer days. After such a long way down, it would be lovely to book a room for the night at the creekside Phantom

ALTERNATIVE ROUTE

The four-to-five-day Thunder River–Deer Creek wilderness loop also descends from the North Rim but is much more challenging and should be attempted only by experienced backpackers who are acclimated to canyon hiking. The rewards are a mystical passage through the famous Narrows and access to one of the park's most enchanting waterfalls.

ABOVE: **It's possible to spot an elk in the canyon in the quieter winter months.**

OPPOSITE: **Hikers might pass rafters camping on the banks of the Colorado River.**

Ranch, a historic oasis designed in 1922 by architect Mary Jane Colter. But lodge rooms are so coveted that the 13-month-advance reservations sell out within minutes of becoming available. (It's essential to secure backcountry permits to camp at a designated campground along the way.)

A short 1.7-mile hike from Phantom Ranch on the River Trail, which crosses the 500-foot-long Silver Bridge (one of only two bridges in the park that span the Colorado River), leads to the Bright Angel Trail and a 4,400-foot climb to the South Rim. Save some energy: Most of the trail's elevation change takes place in the upper four miles. Take a break at the campground at Havasupai Gardens, the traditional land of Native people since time immemorial—the last Havasupai resident, Captain Burro, was forcibly removed in 1928. After a rest in this historic land, you'll begin the climb up the long, seemingly endless series of switchbacks to the canyon rim, at 6,860 feet.

ARIZONA

ARIZONA NATIONAL SCENIC TRAIL

America's Hot Route

DISTANCE: 800 miles one-way **LENGTH OF TRIP:** 6 to 8 weeks **BEST TIME TO GO:** Spring or fall **DIFFICULTY:** Strenuous

In the 1970s, a Flagstaff school teacher named Dale Shewalter envisioned a trail that connected the entire state of Arizona. In 1985 he took the first step toward turning his dream into a reality and walked from Nogales, on the Mexico border, north to Utah. More than a quarter century later, in 2011, the 800-mile-long border-to-border route was finally completed.

The most remarkable aspect of the national scenic trail is how well it highlights the surprising and wild biodiversity of Arizona. Passing through canyons, over mountains, and across grasslands, and from a low of 1,700 feet along the banks of the Gila River to a high of 9,600 feet on the Kaibab Plateau, it showcases every major western ecosystem. And while Indigenous peoples have been traversing this land for more than 10,000 years, the trail is still very isolated. It goes through only three towns, and 82 percent of the trail is singletrack.

It's also among the few 11 national scenic trails in the U.S. that's open to more than just hikers. The path is maintained for all nonmotorized users, including horseback riders and mountain bikers, the latter of which are rerouted around sections of the trail that pass through designated wilderness, where two-wheeled vehicles are restricted. The philosophy behind

OPPOSITE: Hikers follow a path into the Grand Canyon on a stretch of the Arizona National Scenic Trail.

PAGES 22-23: The 800-mile Arizona National Scenic Trail makes its way through Saguaro National Park, named for its famous cacti.

allowing more than just hikers is to ensure that as many people as possible can have a transformative experience in the Arizona outback. To that end, the Arizona Trail Association has a robust volunteer program, with about 25,000 helpers partaking in trail maintenance annually, and projects like Seeds of Stewardship, which gives local schoolchildren experiences on the trail in hopes of their future involvement. "Our goal is to inspire people to get out there, fall in love with these landscapes, and work to protect it," says Matthew Nelson, executive director of the association.

One might think hiking rim to rim through the Grand Canyon would be the highlight of this trail, but there are so many unsung areas of Arizona to discover, such as the spectacular rock formations of the Gila River Canyons in the middle of the state, where mountain lions, black bears, and coatis roam. Then there's the healthy aspen and pine forest groves of the Huachuca Mountains, which rise to 9,000 feet just north of the Mexico border. Here you'll see a 400-foot-wide section of the incomplete border wall that stands out like a surreal art installation.

KNOW BEFORE YOU GO

In the drying Southwest, water is always an issue. That's why the Arizona Trail Association closely monitors the quality and reliability of every water source within a mile of the trail. It partners with FarOut, an app that gives trail users up-to-date data on all these water sources.

ARIZONA

HANGOVER LOOP

No Regrets the Day After in Sedona

DISTANCE: 8.2-mile loop **LENGTH OF TRIP:** 3 to 5 hours **BEST TIME TO GO:** Year-round **DIFFICULTY:** Strenuous

It took millions of years and a multitude of geologic events to create the 25-square-mile oasis of deep red mesas, buttes, spires, and monoliths that surround Sedona. There's no better way to enjoy these splendors than by hiking the 200 trails that meander more than 400 miles through the city and into Coconino National Forest. There's not a bad path in the bunch, but even in this near-mythical land, one hike stands out: It's called Hangover for a reason.

The lollipop-shaped loop is a combination of three vastly different trails: Munds Wagon, Cow Pies, and Hangover. Among mountain bikers, Hangover is known as one of the top three most challenging trails in Sedona because a portion of the singletrack has a sheer wall on one side and a plunging cliff on the other. Then it flows into a steep section of red rock where there is no trail at all. It's also a challenge for hikers, even if they're traversing the trail on two steady feet. Only a series of white paint dots ensure hikers they are going in the right direction. Even on foot, portions of this hike are dangerous, but it's entirely possible—and worth the effort—for those who hike with a partner and pay attention to footing.

Start at the Munds Wagon trailhead east of uptown Sedona in Coconino National Forest. The eponymous trail has been in use for more than a century, originally as one of the most popular cattle trails across the mountains for ranchers in the late 1800s. This hike doesn't go that far, but it still

OPPOSITE: The Hangover Loop is popular with experienced mountain bikers and hikers.

PAGES 26-27: Winter dusts Schnebly Hill in Coconino National Forest with snow.

meanders up and then down into a deep wash lined by junipers, piñon pines, scrub oaks, and agaves just below a popular four-wheel vehicle road before climbing again to the turnoff for the Cow Pies Trail.

The short Cow Pies section leads to one of Sedona's famed vortexes (mythical centers of energy), this one a flat red-rock ledge that sits high over the valley with sweeping views to the west and the 5,440-foot Merry-Go-Round, a limestone and sandstone formation that resembles an old-fashioned carnival ride, to the east. To the north is a sheer wall of red rock and the beginning of the Hangover Trail, where a sign reads "Caution" followed by two black diamonds, similar to what you'd see on expert-only ski trails. Here it's hike at your own risk through steep and spectacular terrain. Be on high alert and make way for mountain bikers, who travel the globe to ride this extreme route. Take it slow and rest assured you'll eventually descend back to the safety of the Munds Wagon Trail.

CULTURAL HIGHLIGHT

What is a vortex, anyway? Many Indigenous groups consider the entire red rock region surrounding Sedona to be sacred, but the four to seven modern-day vortexes originated during the 1980s New Age movement. They are thought to be places where energy emanates from the earth that can heal and enhance self-discovery and spiritual growth.

ARIZONA

HEART OF ROCKS LOOP

A Mystical Hike Through Hoodoos in Chiricahua National Monument

DISTANCE: 7.6-mile loop **LENGTH OF TRIP:** 4 to 6 hours **BEST TIME TO GO:** Spring or fall
DIFFICULTY: Moderate

Thirty-five miles south of I-10 and the closest major town of Wilcox, Arizona, Chiricahua National Monument sits at a unique biological crossroads. Here, the Rocky Mountains meet the Sierra Madre Occidental, and the Chihuahuan Desert meets the Sonoran Desert. From the hiking trails, visitors can see that it's a "crazy, mixed-up kind of place that's not anything like Phoenix," says park ranger Suzanne Moody.

Along the Heart of Rocks Loop, the most strenuous trail in Chiricahua National Monument, hikers will plunge into wild geology, plus take in sweeping views of New Mexico and Arizona, and likely spot a ubiquitous red-tailed hawk. They'll also find hundreds of impossibly balanced rocks and high pinnacles that powerfully demonstrate how ice and water can sculpt the volcanic ash deposits known as rhyolite. Gazing at the unique formations, hikers don't need much of an imagination to see the waterfowl-like shape in Duck on a Rock, the bickering puppet forms in Punch and Judy, or the distinguished elderly woman carved in Old Maid. They do, however, need strong legs to power up almost 1,000 feet of elevation on the well-maintained trail, which was built by the Civilian Conservation Corps in the 1930s, when wild flocks of thick-billed parrots still lived here (the last parrot was seen in 1995).

OPPOSITE: Take in the hoodoos from the top of Chiricahua National Monument.

CALIFORNIA

LOST COAST TRAIL

A Sliver of Sand From Mattole Beach to Shelter Cove

DISTANCE: 24.6 miles one-way **LENGTH OF TRIP:** 2 to 4 days **BEST TIME TO GO:** Spring or fall
DIFFICULTY: Moderate

In Northern California, nestled between the 4,000-foot peaks of the King Range and the crashing Pacific Ocean surf is a stretch of black sand, gravel, and cobblestone known as the Lost Coast. This "trail" is unlike any other in the United States in that it offers access to a remote stretch of coastline full of wildlife, from bobcats and black bears to sea lions and elephant seals; the historic Punta Gorda Lighthouse, which was built in 1912 and refurbished in 2022; and a remarkable quilt of wildflowers on the bluffs.

One might expect a beach hike to be an easy barefoot stroll, but "the Lost Coast is better suited for logistical masterminds as opposed to first-time backpackers," says King Range National Conservation Area ranger Kacie Hallahan. That's largely because of the maritime climate's unpredictable and hypothermia-inducing weather, but also, and even more important, because the tides here are no joke. There are three "impassable zones" on this section of the Lost Coast, the longest of which is five miles, and all can be deadly to navigate at high tides, which can reach three feet or higher. Before you go, learn how to read a National Oceanic and Atmospheric Administration tide table and time your hike appropriately. Hit the tides incorrectly and you could be stranded or swept away. If you need a break, hike up and away from shore to camp.

OPPOSITE: **The Lost Coast Trail follows the shoreline in the King Range National Conservation Area.**

CALIFORNIA

HALF DOME

Steep and Spectacular

DISTANCE: 14 miles round-trip **LENGTH OF TRIP:** 12 hours **BEST TIME TO GO:** Summer to early fall
DIFFICULTY: Strenuous

In 1869 California state geologist Josiah Whitney deemed Half Dome "perfectly inaccessible, being probably the only one of all the prominent points about Yosemite which has never been and will never be trodden by human foot."

More than 150 years later, as many as 300 people per day attempt to prove him wrong by securing a coveted permit to summit this granite behemoth that rises 4,737 feet above Yosemite Valley, despite extreme risks of exposure to rain, wind, and lightning at such heights. Make no mistake: It's no easy feat. In 2024, an experienced 20-year-old hiker fell to her death after slipping on wet granite while ascending the cabled portion. Still, some 50,000 people summit Half Dome every year.

Hiking Half Dome can be dangerous, but this path also leads to some of the most sublime views within Yosemite National Park. Hikers ascend stone steps to the tops of two massive cascades, Vernal and Nevada Falls, before the notoriously steep and scary ascent, which includes a 400-foot stretch of steel cables to assist them above the tree line to the summit. (Note: The cables are only up between Memorial Day and early October.) At the top, hikers find a heavenly perch from which to take in the surrounding peaks of the Sierra Nevada and the lush valley below.

Be forewarned: The cables are precarious in rain and lightning, so start before dawn and turn around at any sign of inclement weather. Permits are available to day hikers in March through a lottery system. Backpackers can request a Half Dome permit in addition to their wilderness permit.

OPPOSITE: Metal cables help hikers ascend the last 400 feet to the summit of Half Dome.

CALIFORNIA

BAY AREA RIDGE TRAIL

A Wild Urban Oasis

DISTANCE: 410 miles round-trip **LENGTH OF TRIP:** 3 to 4 weeks **BEST TIME TO GO:** Year-round
DIFFICULTY: Moderate

In the 1960s, William Penn Mott, Jr., who would become director of the National Park Service, envisioned a 550-mile trail connecting the ridgelines surrounding the San Francisco Bay Area. This may sound straightforward until one realizes that the circumnavigation is almost equivalent to the distance between San Francisco and San Diego.

Mott's dream caught on, and today more than 410 miles of the hiking, cycling, and equestrian trail are complete, connecting iconic landscapes in and around San Francisco. The trail is considered 70 percent complete, but it could take another 20 years to finish Mott's 550-mile vision. To the north are ridgelines overlooking the vineyards of Sonoma and Napa, redwood forests, and Pacific views from the Marin Headlands. Heading south across the Golden Gate Bridge, hikers will pass through the Presidio and Golden Gate Park. Then past San Jose, the trail summits Mount Umunhum, with views of the entire South Bay, before turning north again to traverse the grassy hills of the East Bay.

To mirror the diversity of the urban areas the path crosses, the Bay Area Ridge Trail Council partners with groups such as Latino Outdoors, Outdoor Afro, and Together Bay Area "to get people who have been historically marginalized out there into these really beautiful spaces," says Alex Sabo, advocacy and outreach manager for the council.

OPPOSITE: The Bay Area Ridge Trail affords views of the Santa Cruz Mountains and Pacific Ocean.

CALIFORNIA

SIERRA HIGH ROUTE

A Storied Wilderness to Yourself

DISTANCE: 195 miles one-way **LENGTH OF TRIP:** 12 to 20 days **BEST TIME TO GO:** July to September
DIFFICULTY: Strenuous

More of a rough sketch than a physical tread, high routes are next-level adventures, offering experienced hikers an opportunity to hone skills like route finding while testing the limits of their endurance. Winding north to south along the Sierra Nevada Range through the most storied high-alpine terrain in California, including Sequoia and Kings Canyon National Parks, the John Muir Wilderness, the Ansel Adams Wilderness, and Yosemite National Park, the Sierra High Route is a universe unto itself. The first known high route in the U.S., it was brought to life by legendary climber and historian Steve Roper, whose 1982 *Timberline Country: The Sierra High Route* remains the definitive guide for the trek.

There's a lot to be said for getting off the beaten path: The signs of humanity diminish, there's an expansiveness that doesn't exist on a well-trodden path, and the vistas from on high are like an endless series of Ansel Adams photographs. Most of the Sierra High Route stays between 9,500 and 11,500 feet, a zone of alpine lakes, tundra, and white bark pines, with an array of peaks in the distance backlit by a dusty rose alpenglow. At this altitude, the snow can stick around even into July and arrive as early as September, but the Sierra Nevada has the sunniest, mildest climate of any major mountain range in the world. Intense cerulean skies are the default throughout the summer.

OPPOSITE: **Make camp—and leave no trace behind—near Mammoth Lakes, California.**

PAGES 38-39: **Time your trek for sunrise views over Bullfrog Lake in Kings Canyon National Park.**

There is a price to pay for this quality solitude, however: Mile per mile the Sierra High Route demands twice as much vertical gain and loss as the Pacific Crest Trail (page 46), much of which is a Class III scramble (moderate, steep terrain requiring handholds) across loose scree and precariously tilted boulders. Plus, 100 miles of this route are entirely off-trail—there are no worn paths or signs giving hikers an indication of which direction to go, making it critical to make correct navigational decisions with every step.

Is this extremely rugged adventure worth the effort when there are other ways to access the High Sierra? For experienced hikers, the answer is an unequivocal yes, says professional backpacker Andrew Skurka, who first attempted the route in 2008 and has since guided hundreds of other hikers through this extreme playground of granite basins, serrated peaks, and frosty lakes. "I've always looked at this trip as more of 'What can I learn, what can I gain, and how can I be better on the other side?'" Skurka, the author of *The Ultimate Hiker's Gear Guide,* says. "This is next-level backpacking for people who want to keep learning."

ALTERNATIVE ROUTE

The 215-mile John Muir Trail parallels the Sierra High Route at a lower elevation. While still a challenge—it connects Yosemite National Park to 14,505-foot Mount Whitney, the highest peak in the continental U.S.—it does follow a well-trodden path and offers access to classic High Sierra scenery.

CALIFORNIA AND NEVADA

TAHOE RIM TRAIL

A High Sierra Circumnavigation Like No Other

DISTANCE: 165 miles round-trip **LENGTH OF TRIP:** 10 to 15 days **BEST TIME TO GO:** Late August to early September **DIFFICULTY:** Moderate

The obvious attraction to the Tahoe Rim Trail is that it circumnavigates one of the most stunning lakes on the planet. Sprawling across 122,000 acres, Lake Tahoe is the largest alpine body of water in North America, ringed by the snowcapped Sierra Nevada to the west and its spur, the Carson Range, to the east. At two million years old, Lake Tahoe is also one of the oldest lakes on the planet. The body of water hikers see today is roughly the same size it was a million years ago. And for millennia it has been the geographic and spiritual center for ancestors of the Washoe (Wá·šiw) people of California and Nevada.

Today the Washoe share it with more than 700,000 annual users, who hike, mountain bike, or even e-bike at least a portion of the trail, which crosses two states, two wilderness areas, two state parks, a national forest, and four different ranger districts. Despite the traffic, it's still a good choice for beginning thru-hikers because the trail is a giant circle, eliminating logistical challenges posed by a point-to-point adventure. With its 12 major trailheads spaced every 10 to 15 miles, there are plenty of opportunities to resupply—the trail passes through Tahoe City and dips to within at least five miles of a major town at three other points, ensuring that a fresh pizza or an evacuation, if necessary, is never more than a few hours away.

THE CHALLENGE

Lake Tahoe suffers from extreme overuse. After the July 4, 2023, weekend, volunteers cleaned up 8,559 pounds of trash left behind by revelers on six beaches, including tents, food, beer cans, and human feces. It is imperative that hikers follow "leave no trace" ethics and pack out everything they bring in.

OPPOSITE: While the lake is almost always in view, the Tahoe Rim Trail offers plenty of shade among the trees.

PAGES 42–43: Watch the sunrise over Emerald Bay from the upper portion of Lower Eagle Falls in California.

"It kind of brings the frontcountry to the backcountry," says Anthony Porter of the Tahoe Rim Trail Association, the nonprofit that maintains and manages the trail. "We pride ourselves on how nicely it's maintained," he says, adding that the trail is roughly nine miles longer than its official 165 miles because of rerouting due to damage from a devastating 2021 fire.

With awe-inspiring views almost everywhere, there's no bad place to begin, but most thru-hikers save the Desolation Wilderness for last, setting out from Tahoe City on the lake's northwestern shore and hiking clockwise. This means they'll summit the highest point, 10,338-foot Relay Peak, early on before descending into Nevada, passing historic mining flumes, dense forests, and alpine meadows of lush yellow mule-ears and purple elephant's heads.

Some hikers bring a fishing pole and angle for brown trout at Star Lake, a secluded camping spot at the foot of three of the highest peaks in the Tahoe Basin: Freal, Jobs Sister, and Jobs. Or they fish at one of the many bodies of water in the Lakes

CULTURAL HIGHLIGHT

In addition to trail fundraising, maintenance, and building, the nonprofit Tahoe Rim Trail Association offers hikes led by guides trained in wilderness medicine and mental health emergencies to young people from underrepresented communities. Three children who had been displaced from Afghanistan said that their hike was the best experience of their lives.

ABOVE: **Blue markers help hikers find their way along the rim.**

OPPOSITE: **Hike the trail by the end of September to avoid harsh, albeit beautiful, snowfall.**

Region on the south side of Tahoe Basin, where the trail seems to follow an endless stream of seasonal creeks and lakes. On the west side, the Tahoe Rim and Pacific Crest Trail co-align through the Desolation Wilderness, a High Sierra landscape characterized by granite peaks, glacial lakes, and wind-ravaged pines.

In the height of summer, especially on the weekends near major entry points, the trail can get crowded. But it's a good opportunity to "find a common courtesy," says Porter, "and perpetuate the stewardship method of being nice to the people around you."

To avoid crowds, plan a trip in late May, with the understanding that burrowing through four to five feet of snow in some sections may be a reality. The snow usually melts by the end of June, but some high elevations might have a dusting as late as early August. Snow comes again in late October.

CALIFORNIA TO CANADA

PACIFIC CREST TRAIL

The Wild West

DISTANCE: 2,650 miles one-way **LENGTH OF TRIP:** 5 months **BEST TIME TO GO:** March to September
DIFFICULTY: Moderate

No one has done more to popularize the beauty, solitude, and challenges of the Pacific Crest Trail (PCT) than Cheryl Strayed, who memorialized the epic thru-hike in her 2012 memoir, *Wild: From Lost to Found on the Pacific Crest Trail*. Readers could almost feel the pain from her heavy pack and lacerated blisters. Aches and injuries notwithstanding, Strayed's adventure shined such a spotlight on the longest contiguously developed hiking and equestrian trail in the United States that today roughly 8,000 annual thru-hikers attempt the feat.

Strayed is not the only woman, however, who brought the PCT to life. In 1926, Catherine Montgomery, an educator and avid hiker from Bellingham, Washington, was the first person on record to propose a footpath that ran through the states of California, Oregon, and Washington. But many people were involved in creating the trail, including a group of teenagers known as the YMCA Relay Boys. Over four summers from 1935 to 1938, 40 teams of 14-to-18-year-old boys hiked, explored, and evaluated a route more than 2,000 miles long from Mexico to Canada. Working in 50-mile increments, each team, when finished, would pass off the official logbook to the next group. Today's PCT route still closely resembles the route they mapped almost a century ago.

HISTORICAL FOOTNOTE

Catherine Montgomery, the daughter of Scottish immigrants, is known today as the mother of the Pacific Crest Trail. In 1926 she was the first to champion a western long-distance trail. Way ahead of her time, Montgomery was a single woman, an avid hiker, a suffragist, and a founding faculty member of Western Washington University.

OPPOSITE: Find remarkable views of the northern Sierra Nevada near Donohue Pass.

PAGES 48–49: Catch the sunrise after a night camping at Crater Lake.

In 1968 the PCT and its distinguished eastern sibling, the Appalachian Trail, became the first two of what are now 11 national scenic trails in the United States. But it took 25 more years to fully complete the route, the goal being to intentionally thread it through as many protected areas as possible, showcasing what there is to love about the West, from arid desert to lush rainforest to snow-covered peaks.

In 1993, the entire contiguous PCT from Mexico to Canada was finally, fully finished, crossing 26 national forests, seven national parks, five state parks, and four national monuments. With more elevation gains than any other national scenic trail—489,000 feet—the PCT rises to a high of 13,153 feet at Forester Pass on the border between California's Sequoia and Kings Canyon National Parks and dips to a low of 110 feet at Oregon's Columbia River Gorge. Beyond the physical gains and losses, there are plenty of emotional highs—such as watching a sublime sunrise in the High Sierras after climbing nearly 60,000 feet in 400 miles—and lows, like sweating through extreme desert heat,

KNOW BEFORE YOU GO

Don't be alarmed if your steps are off while thru-hiking the trail. The PCT's stated mileage of 2,650 is inexact. Thanks to the forces of erosion, wildfires, and other factors, sections are constantly being rebuilt. Additionally, the trail has never been mapped with tools that would provide an accurate distance.

ABOVE: **Six-year-old Christian Rego, aka Buddy Backpacker (seen here with his mom, Andrea, and stepdad, Dion, near Ashland, Oregon), became the youngest hiker to complete the Pacific Crest Trail.**

OPPOSITE: **Mountain goats are among the many animals you're likely to see along the thru-hike.**

trekking onward in demanding high altitudes, or shivering through an early season snow.

The trail is well marked, well traveled, and well supported, but it's not easy. To avoid the most extreme heat, thru-hikers start at the southern border with Mexico in late March; to avoid early season snowstorms in Washington's Cascade Range, they aim to be off the trail by late September.

The challenges of the trail are mitigated by its beloved and unofficial army of trail angels, those good folks who seem to show up when hikers most need help, whether in the form of a ride to town or a steaming hot meal. But this is still a wilderness trail, and hikers will often find themselves utterly alone. When the going gets tough, it's essential to relax, take a deep breath, and remember the number one truism of the PCT: "The trail provides."

COLORADO

FOUR PASS LOOP

Rocky Mountain Highs

DISTANCE: 26 miles round-trip **LENGTH OF TRIP:** 3 to 4 days **BEST TIME TO GO:** July to September
DIFFICULTY: Strenuous

For a sense of how majestic the Four Pass Loop is, consider that it cuts through the heart of the Maroon Bells-Snowmass Wilderness, one of only five areas in the entire state of Colorado set aside in the original Wilderness Act of 1964. In the center of the loop are the often snow-covered Maroon Bells, twin siltstone monoliths that rise more than 14,000 feet.

The route is as difficult as it is beautiful. It follows a steep, rocky path, stringing together four passes higher than 12,000 feet. If you're traveling counterclockwise, climbing Buckskin Pass with a full pack is a challenge, but the reward on the other side is Snowmass Lake, a placid mirror at the base of Snowmass Peak that reflects the glory of the surrounding Elk Mountains.

Despite a daunting 11,000-foot elevation gain, the loop has become so popular that in 2023 the U.S. Forest Service implemented a mandatory permit system to limit the number of campers in 15 zones of the Maroon Bells-Snowmass Wilderness. In the Snowmass Lake Zone, one of four permit zones the hike traverses, only 15 groups per night are allowed to camp. This new system has already reduced campsite impact, human waste, tree damage, and human-bear conflict. But it's still the onus of hikers to practice leave-no-trace camping to ensure this wilderness remains pristine.

OPPOSITE: **One of the best parts of the Four Pass Loop: a route through the Maroon Bells-Snowmass Wilderness**

COLORADO

COLORADO TRAIL

From Denver to Durango

DISTANCE: 486 to 491 miles one-way (depending on spur) **LENGTH OF TRIP:** 4 to 6 weeks
BEST TIME TO GO: July to September **DIFFICULTY:** Strenuous

Championed in the early 1970s by a pioneering mountaineer named Gudrun Gaskill, the Colorado Trail was envisioned as a "major intermediate trail," according to a 1974 *Colorado* magazine article, "designed for the less experienced outdoorsman, the person who, like millions of Americans, yearns to get into the mountains but doesn't quite know where or how."

"Intermediate" in this case, however, means a trail that climbs 89,000 feet—more than three Mount Everests—between Denver and Durango, and one in which the average elevation is 10,300 feet. High altitude notwithstanding, the Colorado Trail is theoretically intermediate in that it takes a fraction of the time it does to thru-hike its longer sibling, the Continental Divide Trail (page 80), with which it shares 300 miles. It's also well maintained throughout, thanks to a diligent army of volunteers coordinated by the 50-year-old Colorado Trail Foundation. "We pride ourselves on it being one of the more well-maintained trails in the nation," says its executive director, Paul Talley.

The surrounding landscape is indisputably stunning, but the trail also meanders through historic sites, ski resorts, and small towns of the southern Rocky Mountains. Starting in Waterton Canyon just southwest of Denver, the Colorado Trail climbs to Breckenridge and Copper Mountain, passes west of the Victorian-era mining town of Leadville, and heads under the

KNOW BEFORE YOU GO

The Colorado Trail is beloved by mountain bikers, especially those who take on the annual, beastly Colorado Trail Race in early August. Bikes, however, are not allowed in the six designated wilderness areas the trail traverses—meaning cyclists must detour on dirt roads and add dozens of miles for a grand total of 540.

OPPOSITE: The Colorado Trail passes through the Rocky Mountains, blooming with wildflowers come spring.

PAGES 56-57: Hiking this route in the fall, you'll find golden aspens and mountain views reflected in Twin Lakes.

shadows of the soaring Fourteeners (peaks higher than 14,000 feet) known collectively as the Collegiate Peaks. The trail crests at 13,271 feet near the old mining town of Silverton in the San Juan Mountains and finally descends into the historic railroad hub of Durango.

In its entirety, the trail takes at least a month to tackle, but there are multiple entry points and myriad ways to break up its 28 official sections. One of the most popular routes is the 160-mile Collegiate Loop, which circumnavigates the east and west sides of the Collegiate Peaks, giving hikers an option to summit six Fourteeners—Mounts Yale, Princeton, Antero, and Shavano, and Tabeguache and Huron Peaks—along the way. While a loop, the entire circuit is still all officially on the Colorado Trail because at Twin Lakes Reservoir, southwest of Leadville, it splinters in two before rejoining again south of Salida.

No matter how it's sliced, the trail immerses hikers, mountain bikers, and horseback riders into the Rocky Mountain State's ecosystem, from the hotter, drier ponderosa pine forests of the

BY THE NUMBERS

The Colorado Trail Foundation maintains a robust army of volunteers. In 2024 alone it had:

- **22 trail crews**
- **29 volunteer hours per mile of trail**
- **395 trail crew members**
- **15,000 total number of volunteer hours**
- **$400,000 spent on feeding and providing equipment and supplies to volunteers**

ABOVE: Segment 27 of the Colorado Trail includes seven contiguous miles above the tree line and epic views of the San Juan Mountains.

OPPOSITE: Hike through groves of aspens in Kenosha Pass.

front range to the blue spruce and evergreen forests near Salida to the wildflower-strewn high-alpine meadows of the San Juans.

Because the trail climbs to such high altitudes, snow can be an issue—the reason most hikers wait until early July to tackle a thru-hike. Most attempt it from east to west starting in Denver. Do it in the reverse direction and you'll face monster elevation changes, about 12,000 feet of climbing in 30 miles between Durango and Silverton. While there are no longer any huts along the Colorado Trail, there are ample opportunities for resupply.

Best of all, there's a unique group of trail angels in Lake City, at the end of the longest section of trail without resupply. They can be found every Sunday evening between early July and late August at the Presbyterian Annex serving a hearty and 100 percent free potluck for hikers. Don't even try to leave a tip. Donations from thru-hikers are not accepted.

COLORADO

LONGS PEAK

On Top of the World in Rocky Mountain National Park

DISTANCE: 15 miles round-trip **LENGTH OF TRIP:** 10 to 15 hours **BEST TIME TO GO:** July to September
DIFFICULTY: Strenuous

Of Colorado's 58 Fourteeners—peaks higher than 14,000 feet—Longs Peak is ranked 15th and is a prize for aspiring mountaineers, thanks in part to the long list of legendary figures who have reached its football field–size summit. They include Major John Wesley Powell, the first non-Indigenous person to reach the top in 1868, and Isabella Bird, who in 1873 became the third woman to ascend, popularizing the climb in her autobiography *A Lady's Life in the Rocky Mountains*. In more recent years, Jim Detterline, a legendary Rocky Mountain National Park climbing ranger, earned the nickname "Mr. Longs Peak" by setting a record of climbing the peak 428 times. As of December 2024, Colorado native Lisa Foster set another record by climbing the peak every month for five consecutive years, at least once with Detterline's widow, Rebecca.

Longs Peak is more extreme than a hike. But the popular Keyhole Route, so named for a break in the ridge that looks as if a giant punched a hole through the rock face, doesn't require technical climbing skills in the summer, the reason it draws 15,000 to 20,000 people a year to attempt a scramble up the precipitous path to the 14,259-foot summit. The first six miles of this route are on a trail. The last mile and a half are a combination of scrambling up narrow ridges, loose rock, and steep slabs. This final section is exposed and vulnerable to quickly shifting weather. To ensure a successful summit bid, come well trained and with proper equipment, check updated route conditions via the national park website, and start the hike before dawn.

OPPOSITE: **Hikers must scramble up the last section of Longs Peak.**

IDAHO

CENTENNIAL TRAIL

An Adventure Back to the 19th Century

DISTANCE: 995.6 miles one-way **LENGTH OF TRIP:** 60 days **BEST TIME TO GO:** July to September
DIFFICULTY: Strenuous

Designated in 1990 to commemorate Idaho's 100th anniversary, this remarkably beautiful yet rugged south-to-north traverse starts near the Nevada border at Murphy Hot Springs and winds through 11 national forests and three wilderness areas before ending at the Snake River near Glenns Ferry.

With parts far off the beaten path and little budget to maintain them, the Centennial Trail offers immense beauty, challenging terrain, and the opportunity to see this mountainous state as settlers did more than a century ago. Sagebrush-strewn desert evolves into the jagged 9,000-foot peaks of the Sawtooth Wilderness, which makes its way to the Frank Church–River of No Return Wilderness, where the path follows the mesmerizing canyons of the Salmon River's Middle Fork. (You'll see plenty of rafters making their way along the whitewater here.)

In the Selway-Bitterroot Wilderness, the trail gets rough and has little signage, so hikers need good navigational skills to eventually reach the northern terminus along the Priest River, where the forest alongside the trail turns lush and green.

Hailey Brookins, one of the fewer than 100 confirmed Centennial thru-hikers, completed her epic adventure in 56 days. She sums the trail up this way: "It's very taxing. This is big wilderness."

OPPOSITE: The sun rises above the Salmon River near Camp Ferry.

IDAHO TO MONTANA

PACIFIC NORTHWEST TRAIL

Charismatic Megafauna Along the Canadian Border

DISTANCE: 1,248 miles one-way **LENGTH OF TRIP:** 70 days **BEST TIME TO GO:** July to September
DIFFICULTY: Strenuous

For a sense of how difficult the Pacific Northwest Trail (PNT) is, consider that an average of about 75 thru-hikers complete it per year, compared with the 8,000 or so who thru-hike the Pacific Crest Trail (PCT). The PNT may be more than 1,000 miles shorter than the PCT, but it's also quite a bit more challenging—from the miles-long unfinished sections that require scrambling and bushwhacking through the woods to the coastal Pacific sections that require knowledge of tide tables.

The trail, which starts in the Northern Rockies at Glacier National Park and climbs over five other mountain ranges before ending at Cape Alava in Olympic National Park, is a greater challenge physically and mentally than most other national scenic trails. The payoff, however, is the opportunity to travel through wild terrain, much of which follows the Canadian border, where a large concentration of charismatic megafauna—grizzly bears, wolves, mountain lions, and moose—still live.

Because the PNT is so remote, far north, and physically demanding—many days require more than 5,000 feet of climbing—it requires more planning to hike than most trails do. There are far fewer towns, trailheads, and trail angels along the way to help should you get lost or injured.

OPPOSITE: **Find yourself in another world hiking through the Hoh Rainforest in Olympic National Park in Washington State.**

MONTANA

THE BEATEN PATH

Beauty and Solitude North of Yellowstone National Park

DISTANCE: 26 miles **LENGTH OF TRIP:** 1 to 4 days **BEST TIME TO GO:** July to September
DIFFICULTY: Moderate

Glance at a topographic map of southwestern Montana's Absaroka-Beartooth Wilderness north of Yellowstone National Park and you could almost mistake it for a map of Minnesota's Boundary Waters Canoe Area Wilderness—there's water everywhere. Many of these lakes—Fossil, Fulcrum, Skull, Ouzel, Russell, and plenty others—lie along the Beaten Path, a singular trail made by linking together the Russell Creek and East Rosebud Trails. By no means undiscovered, the Beaten Path is the most well-traveled trail in the wilderness, but it's exponentially less crowded and arguably more stunning than any hike in neighboring Yellowstone.

In addition to the abundance of water, the trail bisects the heart of the Absaroka-Beartooth Wilderness, the traditional homeland of the Apsáalooké, or Absaroka, people—meaning "children of the large-beaked bird." (European settlers mistook the large-beaked bird in question to be a crow, which is how the Apsáalooké became the Crow, but in fact the bird was the mythical thunderbird.) This million-acre wilderness is where two mountain ranges come together—the volcanic Absarokas and the granitic Beartooths—for a total of 120 peaks that are higher than 10,000 feet. Everywhere you look, there's an alpine vista, whether it's 11,699-foot Pilot Peak in the Absaroka range, with its unmistakable profile, or the highest

CULTURAL HIGHLIGHT

While only 26 miles apart by foot, the trailheads for the Beaten Path—East Rosebud and Clarks Fork—lie hundreds of road miles apart via the Beartooth Highway, a spectacular drive that reaches 10,947 feet. To save time, many hikers swap cars with hikers that begin on the other end.

OPPOSITE: Make your way along the trail into Montana's rugged wilderness.

PAGES 68–69: Enjoy lake views in the Absaroka-Beartooth Wilderness.

mountain in the state of Montana: 12,799-foot Granite Peak in the Beartooth range.

The entire route feels straight out of a benevolent fairy tale. Most hikers start at the north end of the trail at the East Rosebud trailhead because the scenery on this side is otherworldly, especially where Impasse Falls flows into Duggan Lake, where anglers feel the spray of the cascade as they cast for cutthroat. Other highlights along the trail include towering lodgepole pine forests, ample opportunity to cast for trout, and space and privacy to pitch a tent, kick back, and gaze out at a wall of peaks. Plus you'll have the satisfaction of reaching the high point of the hike, which is marked by a rock cairn in Fossil Lake, at 10,000 feet, surrounded by the exposed, wildflower-dotted high-alpine tundra of the Beartooth Plateau.

Because the Beaten Path is well marked and easy to follow, it's not uncommon to see minimalist hikers or trail runners trying to pound out a personal best and finishing the entire distance in one fell swoop before nightfall. But it makes no sense to take this hike fast—there are too

GEOLOGY 101

The Beartooth Mountains are home to the highest 41 peaks in Montana. The plateaus, alpine cirques, U-shaped valleys, and lakes of this range were formed by glaciers, 700 of which remain, remnants of the last glacial advance, which ended roughly 19,000 years ago.

many huckleberries to pick, too many trout to catch, too many peaceful campsites at which to relax, and too many beautiful vistas to see. For experienced hikers with a map and compass or GPS, the trail is merely a jumping-off point into a much wilder universe. At least a dozen lakes lie just beyond the Beaten Path and are reachable via an informed scramble or bushwhack.

What really sets this hike apart, however, is that the Absaroka-Beartooth Wilderness is an integral part of the Greater Yellowstone Ecosystem, home to spectacular animals including grizzly bears, elk, deer, moose, mountain goats, bighorn sheep, lynx, and wolves. And while hikers are more likely to see a marmot or a pika than a wolf or a grizzly bear, it's still essential to take precautions and to hike with bear spray close at hand and ready to deploy.

ABOVE: **Cast a line for Yellowstone cutthroat trout in the lakes.**

OPPOSITE: **Rimrock Lake pools more than seven miles from the northern trailhead.**

NEW MEXICO

ALKALI FLAT TRAIL

Sifting Through Gypsum Dunes in White Sands National Park

DISTANCE: 5-mile loop **LENGTH OF TRIP:** 2 to 4 hours **BEST TIME TO GO:** Year-round
DIFFICULTY: Strenuous

Set in the Tularosa Basin under the shadow of the San Andres Mountains of southern New Mexico are 275 square miles of white gypsum sand dunes shimmering beneath a cerulean sky. White Sands National Park protects more than half of this surreal landscape, which may at first seem devoid of life. Get to know it, however, and the Chihuahuan Desert ecosystem comes alive with 220 species of birds, including the great horned owl, exotic reptiles like the bleached earless lizard, and elusive nocturnal mammals such as the bobcat.

Hikers can immerse themselves in this otherworldly park by hiking the loop trail that begins at the end of the eight-mile-long park road. The treadless "trail" shifts with the wind, following red-topped posts up and over the steep white dunes to Alkali Flat, the dry lake bed that was once 1,600-square-mile Lake Otero during the last ice age.

The hike alone is challenging, made more so in spring, which can bring disorienting winds, and in summer, when temperatures can exceed 100°F with no water or shade along the trail. It's also wise to avoid strange-looking objects—they may be unexploded ordnance from nearby White Sands Missile Range, where, in 1945, the world's first atomic bomb was detonated. The range, just 4.4 miles from the national park, is still actively used as a test site by the U.S. Army.

OPPOSITE: **Half the fun of hiking the dunes is running, sliding, or boarding back down.**

NEW MEXICO

PUEBLO ALTO TRAIL

The Heart of an Ancient People

DISTANCE: 5.5-mile loop **LENGTH OF TRIP:** 2 to 3 hours **BEST TIME TO GO:** Spring or fall
DIFFICULTY: Moderate

Tucked away in the northwest corner of New Mexico, Chaco Culture National Historical Park is far off the beaten path from any interstate or major city. But the ruins that sit at 5,000 feet in this high-desert landscape, surrounded by mountains, canyons, and mesas, were once the center of the ancestral Puebloan world. Chaco is still a sacred place revered by 20 affiliated tribes—including the Hopi, Navajo, Ute, Jicarilla Apache, Mescalero Apache, and, especially, the modern Puebloan people—whose ancestors settled here around A.D. 850 and began to plan and build monumental structures.

The centerpiece of the park is Pueblo Bonito, a great house constructed in stages between 850 and 1150 that's believed to have been used for ceremonies, trading, and administrative activities. Covering three acres with nearly 800 rooms, it was the largest building in the United States until the 19th century. Dozens of great houses in Chaco Canyon, the ruins of many still intact, were connected by roads to more than 150 communities throughout the region.

There is no better way to see the sweeping scope of the Chaco world than by hiking the Pueblo Alto Trail. The 5.5-mile backcountry loop offers a dramatic look—from a mesa 600 feet above the ancient city—at the buildings (many called "great houses") and surrounding infrastructure

KNOW BEFORE YOU GO

This is a remote backcountry park that requires travel on unpaved, rutted, rocky roads that can be impassable when wet or snowy. It's wise to call the visitors center for a road report and bring a paper map (GPS is unreliable). And always be respectful, because the roads pass through private tribal land.

OPPOSITE: A rock cairn sits in view of the Fajada Butte at Chaco Culture National Historical Park.

PAGES 76-77: Clear skies above Casa Rinconada and other ancestral Puebloan sites in Chaco Canyon make for optimal stargazing.

that tied this community of roughly 3,000 people together.

The hike begins with a steep and dramatic climb up a rocky slope and through a crack in the canyon wall as wide as the average adult's arm span. Once on top of the mesa, hikers traveling counterclockwise can follow the rim and view Pueblo Bonito and the second largest great house, Chetro Ketl, with features such as a three-story great kiva and an elevated plaza. From this height, especially at certain times of day, visitors can see how all these buildings were oriented toward the sun, moon, and cardinal directions.

Hikers will also pass Jackson's Stairway, a series of footholds carved into the sandstone cliff face of the mesa that were used to descend to the canyon floor. The "staircase" was rediscovered in the 1800s by William Henry Jackson, a photographer for the U.S. Geological and Geographic Survey of the Territories. Along the northern segment of the loop, hikers can see a trace of the Great North Road that once connected Chaco to other communities,

HISTORICAL FOOTNOTE

Millions of years before the Chacoan people arrived, the site of their ancient city was at the edge of an inland sea where fierce creatures known as mosasaurs and plesiosauri hunted fish. Many fossilized remains of this era have been found at Chaco, including jawbones and teeth.

ABOVE: **Pottery pieces can be seen along the trail—leave them where they are, as they're significant to ancestral and modern Puebloans.**

OPPOSITE: **Walk back in time through the dwellings of ancestral Puebloans.**

like the great house at what is now Aztec Ruins National Monument, 69 miles north.

Some lucky hikers will even see pottery sherds, many of which sit where the ancestral Puebloan people left them millennia ago. These artifacts are considered by modern Puebloan people to be part of their ancestors' spirits, so it's essential to leave them exactly where they are and not, as some visitors do, build pottery-sherd cairns or take them home as souvenirs.

One of the most thrilling aspects for visitors to Chaco Culture National Historical Park is being able to independently wander through the remains of this ancient city, seeing the brilliance of a civilization that has withstood the test of time. When the sun sets below the western horizon, the ink-black night sky begins to twinkle with stars, planets, and constellations seen by those who came before.

NEW MEXICO TO MONTANA

CONTINENTAL DIVIDE TRAIL

Where the Waters Part Ways

DISTANCE: 3,100 miles one-way **LENGTH OF TRIP:** 5 months **BEST TIME TO GO:** Northbound in April; southbound in June or July **DIFFICULTY:** Strenuous

The spine of North America spans 3,100 miles from the endangered Chihuahuan Desert in New Mexico to the Crown of the Continent in Montana. In between lie the New Mexico Mountains, Colorado Plateau, Southern Rockies, Wyoming Basin, Greater Yellowstone Ecosystem, and the Middle Rockies. The Continental Divide Trail is the place from which water emerges and flows west to the Pacific or east to the Arctic or Atlantic Oceans and has been a migration corridor for humans and animals for thousands of years.

In the 1960s, the bones of what would become the Continental Divide Trail (CDT) were known as the "Blue Can Trail," so named because volunteers from the Rocky Mountain Trails Association nailed blue-painted tuna cans to trees to mark the original route for approval by the Forest Service. The first segment of the trail, between the town of Empire, Colorado, and Rocky Mountain National Park, was established in 1962. It would take 16 more years for it to officially become a national scenic trail in 1978.

Unlike what its name suggests, the CDT does not traverse the harrowing spine of the Continental Divide. It does, however, shadow the entire 3,100-mile distance and includes a dramatic matrix of landscapes that weaves through communities and cultures like a living history museum.

"The way we view it is that the trail has connected people to life since

HISTORICAL FOOTNOTE

Of the three trails that make up the Triple Crown of hiking—the Appalachian Trail (AT), the Pacific Crest Trail (PCT), and the Continental Divide Trail (CDT)—the CDT was the last to be established as a national scenic trail. It was designated in 1978, a decade after the AT and PCT.

OPPOSITE: Set up camp on a ridgeline in San Juan National Forest, near Durango, Colorado.

PAGES 82-83: For lake and mountain sunset views, make camp at Wyoming's Island Lake in the Wind River Range.

time immemorial," says Teresa Ana Martinez, executive director and co-founder of the Continental Divide Trail Coalition. "It's not just the tread; it's the whole landscape that people are experiencing."

The actual tread consists of mostly 18-to-24-inch singletrack, some two-track Forest Service roads, and 167 miles of pavement that will eventually be rerouted to new sections of trail. In New Mexico, it climbs the flanks of Mount Taylor, a dormant stratovolcano that is sacred to the Navajo, the Pueblo, and many Apache. At Alice Creek, north of Lincoln, Montana, the trail passes a 10,000-year-old campsite used by Indigenous people who traversed this intersection between the plains and the highlands to hunt elk and buffalo. Hikers can still see marks from their travois, a sled made of two poles strapped to a horse or a dog.

The CDT also passes critical points in the creation of the United States, co-aligning in New Mexico with El Camino Real de Tierra Adentro National Historic Trail, the remains of an important north-to-south trade route during the

CULTURAL HIGHLIGHT

More than 1,000 years ago, the Zuni and Acoma Pueblo people built a trail with stone bridges and way-finding cairns to connect their two communities. The 7.5-mile trail, which traverses the hardened lava flows of New Mexico's El Malpais National Monument, is the one still used by CDT hikers today.

Spanish Colonial era that started in Mexico City. At 7,373-foot Lemhi Pass in Montana, hikers can stand where Meriwether Lewis (of Lewis and Clark fame) departed from the main group and came in contact with members of the Shoshone Tribe outside U.S.-controlled territory.

Total elevation gain on the CDT is a whopping 457,000 feet, but the trail is not all about climbing. There is a diverse blend of landscapes, like in the boot heel of New Mexico where the trail starts in the arid Chihuahuan Desert under a sky so dark that the stars sparkle like diamonds. In Colorado, hikers will eventually summit 14,278-foot Grays Peak, the highest point on any national scenic trail; and farther north in Wyoming, they'll walk right past Old Faithful geyser in Yellowstone National Park. Northbound thru-hikers will complete their trek at the lowest elevation on the entire trail: 4,200 feet at Waterton Lake in Glacier National Park.

ABOVE: The Continental Divide Trail is long and grueling, but opportunities to stop and rest abound, including at Summit Lake in Wyoming.

OPPOSITE: Flowers bloom in front of snow-dusted peaks in Wyoming's Titcomb Basin.

NEVADA

BRISTLECONE PINE GLACIER TRAIL

A Starkly Beautiful and Surprising Landscape

DISTANCE: 4.8 miles out and back **LENGTH OF TRIP:** 3 to 6 hours **BEST TIME TO GO:** Memorial Day to Labor Day
DIFFICULTY: Moderate

Great Basin National Park is not a place for visitors just passing through—one needs to drive hours out of their way to get here. But the extended road trip is worth the effort. The park has the longest developed cave system in Nevada; sits on the flanks of 13,062-foot Wheeler Peak, the highest mountain in Nevada; and is home to the oldest nonclonal species (not derived from a single cell or single ancestor) on the planet, the Great Basin bristlecone pine.

"This park subverts a lot of people's expectations," says Travis Mason-Bushman, Great Basin's chief of interpretation. "They think it's the desert, like Death Valley, but you're going to find the last glacier between the Rocky Mountains and the Sierra Nevada."

The trail to that glacier starts at 10,000 feet and climbs 600 feet in 1.4 miles to a grove that once held 4,900-year-old Prometheus, a Great Basin bristlecone pine and the oldest-known single organism on Earth until it was cut down by a research student in the 1960s. The exact former location of Prometheus is a secret that is carefully guarded by both the park and modern-day researchers, but hikers can still see other gnarled, twisted living trees that have survived on this windswept mountain for millennia. Continue a mile farther to the rim of Wheeler Peak Glacier, which sits in a glacial cirque abutting a 1,000-foot vertical face of Wheeler Peak.

OPPOSITE: The patriarch of a small bristlecone grove stands tall in Nevada's Great Basin National Park.

OREGON

OREGON COAST TRAIL

Alone Among the Dunes, Sea Stacks, and Upland Forests

DISTANCE: 425 miles one-way **LENGTH OF TRIP:** 3 to 4 weeks **BEST TIME TO GO:** Spring or fall
DIFFICULTY: Easy to moderate

It's easy to love a trail that begins with a 16-mile stroll on a beautiful black sand beach along the crashing Pacific Ocean. The Oregon Coast Trail (OCT), which stretches 425 miles from the mouth of the Columbia River at Fort Stevens State Park and ends at Crissey Field State Recreation Site near the Oregon-California border provides access to one of the most pristine, extended stretches of coastline left in the continental United States.

That this trail exists is thanks to forward-thinking legislators who passed the Oregon Beach Bill of 1967, which officially established a right to what most Oregonians already thought they had—public access to beaches from the water up to 16 vertical feet above the low-tide mark. The act essentially made the coastline one long and skinny 363-mile state park. (Beach access isn't as democratic as one might think: Hawaii is the only other state that secures this right.)

Due to headlands, high tides, and other impediments, it's impossible for the OCT to follow the coastline the entire way. But variety is what makes this thru-hike so compelling. It meanders past massive dunes, multistory sea stacks, historic lighthouses, and skeletal shipwrecks; heads inland on trails through state parks shaded by towering Douglas fir, western red cedar, and Sitka spruce trees; occasionally requires a ferry

POST-HIKE ACTIVITY

With 28 towns along the coastline, many of which contain delightful inns and restaurants, the OCT is akin to an inn-to-inn hike in Europe. Its proximity to civilization is also one of the reasons it is known among thru-hikers as one of the most expensive trails in the U.S.

OPPOSITE: Sea stacks stand tall offshore from Arch Rock State Park.

PAGES 90-91: The verdant Oregon Coast Trail follows the coastline at Sisters Rock State Park.

around bay mouths and headlands; and skirts in and around 28 coastal towns, each with its own personality. There's also the ever present Pacific Ocean, alive with whales, orcas, porpoises, sea lions, seals, and a cacophony of birds—from screaming eagles to squawking Harlequin ducks.

"It's not a wilderness, but it is an adventure," says Bonnie Henderson, who wrote the guidebook *Hiking the Oregon Coast Trail*. Case in point: On one of her adventures along the trail, she was almost stranded after hitching a ride around a bay with a local crabber who mistakenly dropped her off on a sandbar. But thankfully, shortly after he pulled away the crabber noticed that the sandbar was an island, turned around, and ferried Henderson to solid land. "This is not a no-brainer hike—you do have to pay attention," she says.

Hikers also need to understand the tides and carry a tide chart. Many rivers and headlands can be crossed at low tide but become dangerous at high tide, when the water reaches chest height. And while the Oregon Coast is mild and

WILDLIFE SIGHTING

Among the 250-plus species of birds found along the Oregon coast are snowy plovers, which use beaches for nesting March through September. Diminishing in number, these plump little shorebirds are a species of concern (at risk but not yet endangered), so hikers need to walk on wet sand around the nesting areas. Dogs are strictly prohibited.

ABOVE: **The trail passes Heceta Head Lighthouse, opened in 1894, which stands 206 feet above the Pacific Ocean.**

OPPOSITE: **Boardwalks help hikers make their way along the Oregon Coast Trail.**

mostly sunny in the summer months, the Pacific Ocean is never warm and is very dangerous to swim in—rip currents can pull hikers out to sea.

If there's a downside to the OCT, it's that 160 miles of it still follow a road, the majority of which is along the shoulder of U.S. Highway 101, a heavily trafficked route. Hikers can use a public bus, private taxi, or even a ferry in some places, but there are also spots where hiking the shoulder along the highway is unavoidable.

Despite the highway stretches, hikers still find this coastal trail to be exquisite. "When you're out on the coast, you can turn around and see this series of headlands fading off in blue behind you and see how far you've been," Henderson says. "Then you can look ahead to see other headlands stacked up one after the other. It's unusual to see how far you're going and where you've been."

OREGON

TIMBERLINE TRAIL

Coming 'Round the Mountain

DISTANCE: 42 miles one-way **LENGTH OF TRIP:** 1 to 4 days **BEST TIME TO GO:** July to September
DIFFICULTY: Strenuous

Circling the base of 11,239-foot Mount Hood at the tree line, the Timberline Trail has a fierce reputation among backpackers. One might think a circumnavigation would be easier than a summit, but the trail drops steeply, then climbs out of one glacial drainage after another. Within these drainages, especially during spring runoff or after a summer storm, are creeks powerful enough to carry rocks and trees. Bridges don't fare well in such a constantly shifting environment, so hikers are on their own to ford streams that can be five to 15 feet wide.

In addition to a physical challenge, the Timberland Trail offers a spectacular diversity of scenery: On the western flank, you'll hike through lush Cascade forests of Douglas fir, western red cedar, and hemlock, with intermittent peeks at the Portland metro area below and mighty Mount Rainier to the north. On the drier eastern flank, you'll trek through Ponderosa pine forests and grasslands. The trail also provides access to two fascinating historic sites: The first is the Cloud Cap Inn, a onetime fine-dining resort with flush toilets built at 6,000 feet in 1889. The inn was the mountain's first permanent resort, but it closed in 1946. Today, it is used by the Crag Rats mountain-rescue group and is closed to the public except for the occasional tour. The second site, Timberline Lodge, built in 1937, was used as the outer facade for Stanley Kubrick's bloody thriller *The Shining*.

OPPOSITE: Wildflowers bloom in the fields below Mount Hood.

OREGON TO MONTANA

NEZ PERCE (NEE-ME-POO) NATIONAL HISTORIC TRAIL

Commemorating a Tragic Flight

DISTANCE: 1,170 miles one-way; 20.2 miles in Yellowstone National Park **LENGTH OF TRIP:** 1 to 2 days for Yellowstone section
BEST TIME TO GO: June to October **DIFFICULTY:** Moderate

"I am tired; my heart is sick and sad. From where the sun now stands, I will fight no more forever," said Chief Joseph, leader of the Wal-lam-wat-kain band of Nez Perce, following his surrender on October 5, 1877, at Bear Paw battlefield after a nearly 1,200-mile flight from Oregon.

The 1,170-mile-long Nez Perce National Historic Trail commemorates the 126-day journey made by roughly 750 Nez Perce, most of whom were children, women, and elderly, to escape the U.S. Army, which was trying to force the Indigenous people onto a reservation. The present-day route travels from eastern Oregon through central Idaho, south to Yellowstone National Park, and then north again, stopping 40 miles south of Canada where the final battle took place in what would become Montana.

The entire 1,170-mile trail is not maintained for hiking, but one powerful section is the 20.2-mile Mary Mountain–Nez Perce Trail in the heart of Yellowstone National Park. The Nez Perce eluded their captors here but had violent clashes with the visitors to the world's first national park, resulting in two deaths.

No matter where hikers choose to follow it, "we ask that the trail be treated with respect," says enrolled tribal member Sandra Broncheau-McFarland. "The Trail is sacred. It is the dust and blood of our ancestors."

OPPOSITE: Tipi tents are set up on the Lemhi River in Idaho for a reenactment of the 1877 Nez Perce attempt to flee when the U.S. Cavalry forced the Indigenous people onto a reservation.

UTAH

ANGELS LANDING

A Devilish Climb in Zion National Park

DISTANCE: 5.4 miles round-trip **LENGTH OF TRIP:** 4 to 5 hours **BEST TIME TO GO:** Spring or fall
DIFFICULTY: Strenuous

The most famous hike in Zion Canyon was named by Frederick Vining Fisher, a Methodist minister who on a 1916 expedition with two local boys—Ethelbert Bingham and Claud Hirschi—declared the perch atop a Navajo sandstone monolith that rises 1,000 dizzying feet above the Virgin River so sublime that it was only fit for angels. The name stuck. More than a century later, hundreds of people per day—not all of them angels—secure a permit to attempt Angels Landing, a sweaty, nearly 1,500-foot climb to a heavenly oasis atop a sheer cliff dropping to the canyon floor.

It might be surprising that a dramatic landscape of precipitous rock walls could be made into a permanent home. But the Southern Paiute, who called themselves Nungwu ("the people"), lived in this place, which they called Moo Koon Tooh Veap ("earth coming up"), for millennia because the pastel sandstone cliffs provided safety and shelter from weather and enemies and gurgled with freshwater springs and a free-flowing river. Their homeland became considerably less safe, however, when Mormons began to settle in the region in the 1850s, bringing with them epidemics and a thirst for arable land.

By the time Maj. John Wesley Powell arrived on his first scientific expedition to southern Utah in 1872, most of the Southern Paiute had been driven out or killed by epidemics or other violent means. Powell named the canyon Mukuntuweap in their honor and urged the U.S. government to protect it, which President William Howard Taft did in 1909 by creating

KNOW BEFORE YOU GO

When the new lottery was instituted to hike Angels Landing in 2022, the two-tiered system allowed hikers to apply for a permit months in advance or a day before arrival. Depending on the day of the week and the time of the year, between 10 and 100 percent of applicants receive permits.

OPPOSITE: Chains help hikers reach the summit of Angels Landing, but the path is narrow—be mindful of the two-way traffic.

PAGES 100-101: Hike the 21 switchbacks of Walter's Wiggles.

the 16,000-acre Mukuntuweap National Monument. In 1918 the monument became a national park, and a year later its name was changed to Zion, the Mormons' preferred name for the canyon, which means "sanctuary" in ancient Hebrew.

There's time to ponder the canyon's geologic and human history on the hike to Angels Landing, which starts by crossing the Virgin River, then follows the West Rim Trail 1,000 feet up through a serpentine section known as Walter's Wiggles. Built a century ago, thanks to the ingenuity of Walter Ruesch, the park's superintendent in the 1920s, Walter's Wiggles is a series of 21 tight switchbacks that were carved right into the rock. The original switchback route was created in 1926, but in 1985 Walter's Wiggles underwent a resurfacing project that required 258 helicopter flights and mules to carry the 88 cubic yards of concrete needed on the trail.

After making it through Walter's Wiggles, hikers will have an opportunity to rest at Scout Lookout, a roomy perch with a view of the Virgin River, before ascending the steep, half-mile,

ALTERNATIVE ROUTE

In nearby Bryce Canyon National Park, the Queens Gardens and Navajo Combination Loop is also stunning with half the vertical feet of climbing. The 2.9-mile hike descends into Bryce Canyon Amphitheater, where hikers meander around hundreds of strange and wonderful hoodoo formations, such as Thor's Hammer, before climbing 600 feet back out.

ABOVE: From the top of Angels Landing, hikers can take in what feels like all of Zion National Park.

OPPOSITE: The path to Angels Landing is carved right into the cliffside.

knife-edge push to the 5,790-foot summit on a trail that is less than three feet wide in places. A chain handrail helps hikers keep their balance steady when glancing down at the sheer drop-offs on either side.

Before a permitting system for the trail was implemented in 2022, this section often mimicked the conga line of climbers near the summit of Mount Everest. Today, however, the new system equally distributes the absolute maximum limit of hikers per day: 800 to be exact. While these new restrictions have significantly improved hikers' experiences on the trail, some sections have room for only one person, so hikers need to use their most angelic behavior and be considerate of others. Patience pays off. The view from the top is pure heaven, with sun dancing off red canyon walls that were formed by wind and water over millions of years.

UTAH

BUCKSKIN GULCH TO PARIA CANYON

The Heart of Darkness and Light via the Wire Pass Trailhead

DISTANCE: 27 miles out and back **LENGTH OF TRIP:** 1 to 2 days **BEST TIME TO GO:** Spring or fall
DIFFICULTY: Moderate

There are more photographed, easy-to-access slot canyons in the Southwest, but Buckskin Gulch is one of the longest in the world, with uninterrupted narrows for 15 miles that rise to 500 feet in places. The cool, peaceful interior has the atmosphere of a cathedral, one filled with spectacular whorls, precipitous cliffs, and ancient petroglyphs.

The Buckskin trailhead is the official start of the route, but for a more direct, adventurous, and interesting shot into the heart of the slot canyon, start at the Wire Pass trailhead. It requires a rope for lowering gear through some sections that narrow to two feet wide, and in other sections, hikers may need to wade through waist-deep water. But keep claustrophobia in check—at the confluence with Buckskin Gulch, the cliffs open to an oasis of grass, trees, and wildflowers that makes an ideal spot to camp before narrowing again to angular sections where rays of the sun can barely reach the bottom.

The increasingly popular hike requires a permit—the Bureau of Land Management limits access to the canyon to 20 people a day. It's also imperative that hikers check the forecast for rain so as not to get swept away in a powerful rush of raging water carrying rocks and logs.

OPPOSITE: **You may have to wade through ankle-high water, but the red stone walls of Paria Canyon in Vermilion Cliffs National Monument are worth the wet socks.**

UTAH AND ARIZONA

HAYDUKE TRAIL

A Hike Fit for Monkey Wrenchers

DISTANCE: 800 miles one-way **LENGTH OF TRIP:** 40 to 60 days **BEST TIME TO GO:** Spring or fall
DIFFICULTY: Strenuous

Edward Abbey spent two solitary summers in the 1950s working as a ranger at Arches National Monument (before it evolved into a national park). The Pennsylvania native came to understand that there is no better landscape than the Southwest—a place of mind-altering geology, ferocious wide-open spaces, sublime light, and millennia of human history—to find peace in the soul. And what better way to see this vast country than to put one foot in front of the other?

"For godsake folks ... take off those stupid sunglasses and unpeel both eyeballs, look around," wrote the famously recalcitrant monkey wrencher in his 1968 autobiography, *Desert Solitaire: A Season in the Wilderness*. "Throw away those goddamned idiotic cameras! ... Stand up straight like men! Like women! Like human beings! And walk—walk—walk upon our sweet and blessed land!"

In the late 1990s two acolytes, Joe Mitchell and Mike Coronella, heeded Abbey's call, spending months exploring the Colorado Plateau to piece together a route they named the Hayduke Trail in honor of George Washington Hayduke III, the antihero in Abbey's 1975 novel *The Monkey Wrench Gang*. Hayduke, a former Green Beret, explosives expert in the Vietnam War, and militant environmentalist, uses unconventional means, including blowing up the Glen Canyon Dam, to fight for environmental justice.

Much like the fictional Hayduke does, his namesake trail meanders through the most iconic sites in the Southwest, starting in Arches National

HISTORICAL FOOTNOTE

Edward Abbey went down in history as a heroic radical environmentalist who has a cultlike following to this day. In recent decades, however, Abbey has been called out as a racist, misogynist, and arrogant xenophobe. Read Abbey's canon, starting with *Desert Solitaire*, and decide for yourself.

OPPOSITE: Hiking the Hayduke Trail requires careful maneuvering through slot canyons.

PAGES 108-109: Snowshoes are a necessity for hiking majestic Bryce Canyon come winter.

Park in the northeast, then zigzagging through Canyonlands National Park, Glen Canyon National Recreation Area, Capitol Reef National Park, Grand Staircase–Escalante National Monument, and west to Bryce Canyon National Park, before dipping south into the Grand Canyon and taking a sharp turn north to finish in Zion National Park. More of a route than a trail, it's a patchwork of existing paths, dirt roads, and bushwhacking.

"It's a pick-your-own-adventure kind of trail," says Andrew Skurka, a former National Geographic Adventurer of the Year who ended his Hayduke Trail hike on the western boundary of the Grand Canyon. "It's more of a recommendation, like 'if this works for you great, but if you need to resupply or if want to go see something else or need a day to recover and be at lower elevations, you can take this other route' kind of hike."

Intensely rugged, the trail ranges in elevation from 1,800 feet in the Grand Canyon to 11,419 feet at the top of Mount Ellen's south

CULTURAL HIGHLIGHT

In addition to dreaming up the trail and writing its only published guidebook in 2005, trail co-founder Joe Mitchell is a fishing guide and recipient of an Antiquities Award from the Utah State Historical Society. The trail's other co-founder, Mick Coronella, is a wine expert and officer of Utah's Grand County Search and Rescue team.

ABOVE: The Hayduke Trail veers into the Grand Canyon, a great place to stop for a stretch.

OPPOSITE: Before finishing the hike in Zion National Park, some make camp along the Colorado River in Grand Canyon National Park.

summit. While there are difficult sections, especially traversing portions of the Grand Canyon, much of the trail follows relatively flat jeep roads, traverses canyon bottoms, or crosses seemingly endless pasturelands full of cattle and copious amounts of cow pies. The hiking itself may not be terribly strenuous, but the route still poses serious challenges, including finding water, arranging resupply, and timing permits to coincide with the multitude of public lands the trail crosses.

The payoff, however, is having an experience that is exactly what Abbey envisioned: Getting off the beaten path long enough to find an undiscovered pictograph on a canyon wall, watch the orange sun drop below the horizon from a hidden perch in the Grand Canyon, or sleep out under an enormous sky full of brilliant constellations that make you feel like a mere speck in the universe.

WASHINGTON STATE

WONDERLAND TRAIL

A Magical Turn Around Mount Rainier

DISTANCE: 93 miles **LENGTH OF TRIP:** 7 to 14 days **BEST TIME TO GO:** Summer **DIFFICULTY:** Strenuous

Summiting Mount Rainier, the most glaciated peak in the lower 48, has been a prize since the 19th century, when author and mountaineer P. B. Van Trump and his friend Gen. Hazard Stevens made the first recorded ascent in 1870. For the six Native communities—the Nisqually, Puyallup, Squaxin Island, Muckleshoot, Yakama, and Cowlitz—whose traditional lands include the mountain they call Tahoma, Rainier was never a prize to summit. It was a point of awe and reverence. Rarely did these groups climb high on the mountain. Instead, they traveled seasonally to the volcano's flanks, gathering berries, fishing for trout, hunting deer, and partaking in spiritual quests.

For those who choose to climb, it's a rugged ascent that requires traversing glaciers, navigating deep crevasses, and scaling precipitous slopes. The summit of this active volcano has shrunk by nearly 22 feet because of climate change since its official U.S. Geological Survey height of 14,410 feet in 1956, but it is still a hard-won first step for aspiring mountaineers.

On the Wonderland Trail, which circumnavigates Mount Rainier, hikers can get a sense of that abundance and challenge themselves with the immense difficulty that comes with circling a mountain on a path that has a total elevation gain of 24,939 feet, almost twice the height of the summit.

This epic meander not only allows hikers 360-degree views of Mount Rainier but also takes them through slices of heaven on earth. "Having

CONSERVATION HIGHLIGHT

The trail is ringed by subalpine meadows with hundreds of species of wildflowers like glacier lilies, alpine asters, and Jacob's ladders. Because the growing season is so short, the plants need to expend their energy by rapid flowering, so they have limited resources to survive a trampling by an unwitting hiker.

OPPOSITE: The Wonderland Trail makes its way by a small tarn below Curtis Ridge.

PAGES 114-115: Spot Mount Rainier peeking out in the distance on the Cowlitz Divide section of the trail.

hiked most of the long-distance trails in the United States, I can unequivocally say that the Wonderland Trail is the most breathtaking," says Tami Asars, who wrote *Hiking the Wonderland Trail*. "The route unveils the mountain in all its grandeur: ancient, crumbling stone walls, rainbow-colored wildflower meadows, glacial-carved canyons with their turbulent waters, alpine vistas graced by jade lakes and permanent snowfields."

The number one rule of hiking this popular trail is to know what you're getting into. The trail profile has extreme highs (6,700-foot Panhandle Gap) and extreme lows (2,320 feet at Ipsut Creek in the old-growth rainforest of the Carbon Valley). With 18 designated wilderness camps (requiring backcountry-permit reservations plus a national park fee) and four main entry points—Carbon River, Longmire, Sunrise, and Mowich Lake—there's not one right way to do this hike.

No matter where hikers begin, each section of trail is a wonderland unto itself, with highlights like Indian Henry's Hunting Ground,

CULTURAL HIGHLIGHT

In 2024 Mount Rainier National Park hired its first composer in residence, Stephen Lias, whose job it was to hike, camp, and draft compositions to capture the spirit of the mountain in a piece of classical music. The works of the self-styled "adventurer-composer" have been played by symphonies around the United States.

ABOVE: Keep an eye out, and you might be lucky enough to catch sight of a spotted fawn.

OPPOSITE: Cottony bistort blooms among purple and pink wildflowers in Paradise Meadow.

a dubious moniker for a subalpine park in the southwest section of the trail named after a Native man whose given name was Satulik and who guided early climbing parties that included John Muir, James Longmire, and Van Trump. On the mountain's northwest flank, near the Carbon River entrance, the historic Tolmie Peak Fire Lookout was built by the Civilian Conservation Corps in 1933 and is one of only four fire lookouts left in the park. It offers expansive views to Mount St. Helens to the south, the Olympic Mountains to the west, Mount Baker to the north, and massive, hulking Mount Rainier directly to the east. On the north side, the trail skirts the terminal moraine of Winthrop Glacier and winds through rolling meadows sprouting with a riot of wildflowers. To the east is Panhandle Gap, which is often covered in snow through August.

WASHINGTON STATE

HOH RIVER TRAIL

Enchantment in Olympic National Park

DISTANCE: 37 miles round-trip **LENGTH OF TRIP:** 3 to 5 days **BEST TIME TO GO:** June to October
DIFFICULTY: Moderate

This otherworldly out-and-back hike in the heart of Olympic National Park is a quiet, awe-inducing experience. The trail begins in the Hoh, a wild swath of old-growth rainforest, before climbing past the trees and above timberline to Blue Glacier, providing views to Mount Olympus beyond. It's a popular hike, but one in which it's still easy to find peace, first in the understory of the Douglas fir, Sitka spruce, western hemlock, and western red cedar, and later in the high-alpine spaces leading to the glacier.

The English language has too few words to describe the brilliant shades of green that sprout from a rainforest that receives up to 14 feet of annual precipitation. Perpetuating the growth are downed trees, known as nurse logs, which incubate fallen seedlings that would otherwise be smothered by the thick beds of mosses and liverworts blanketing the forest floor.

"The Hoh River Trail offers the opportunity to experience the diverse ecosystems of Olympic National Park," says supervisory interpretive park ranger Jared Lowe. "Towering stands of ancient coniferous trees rich with epiphytes loom over the trail as sounds of the Hoh River echo in the background, a reminder that water and rainfall are in abundance and the primary life-sustaining resource in the Hoh River Valley."

OPPOSITE: Stop to cool down along the Hoh River.

PAGES 120-121: Your hiking pace may slow as you marvel at the Hall of Mosses in the Hoh River Valley.

The trail follows the Hoh River and is relatively flat for almost 13 miles, the point at which many hikers drop off. At this point, the trail starts its nearly 3,500-foot climb over the last five miles, first to the Hoh Bridge, a wooden structure that spans a canyon carved by a rushing creek, and then beyond to moss-fringed Elk Lake and a hazardous rockslide area. Finally, it reaches the last campsite at Glacier Meadows and the first glimpse of Blue Glacier at mile 17.5. The trail ends a mile later at the glacier's lateral moraine, with a view of a white river of ice that appears to be frozen in time. Beyond is the white-capped peak of Mount Olympus.

There's good reason to linger along this trail. The ecosystems it traverses are vestiges of a disappearing era. The Hoh is a well-protected slice of a shrinking forest that once spanned the Pacific coast from southeastern Alaska to the central coast of California. As for the glaciers, it is estimated that they will have entirely disappeared from the Olympic Peninsula by 2070.

WILDLIFE SIGHTING

Olympic National Park is home to the largest unmanaged herd of Roosevelt elk in the Pacific Northwest. Named for President Theodore Roosevelt, the "conservation president," they are also the largest species of elk in North America, with cows that weigh up to 700 pounds and bulls that top the scales at 1,100 pounds.

WYOMING

TETON CREST TRAIL

A Wild Western Classic (From the Top of Jackson Hole Aerial Tram to String Lake)

DISTANCE: 35 miles one-way **LENGTH OF TRIP:** 3 to 5 days **BEST TIME TO GO:** July to September
DIFFICULTY: Strenuous

In the pantheon of classic American hikes, the Teton Crest Trail ranks at the top of the list, thanks to magnificent views to the highest spires in the Teton Range and the opportunity to see megafauna such as moose, deer, grizzly, and elk. "This is one trail that everyone who hikes it is blown away [by]," says former Grand Teton National Park ranger and author Kevin Grange. "The views get better with each mile."

Sections of the trail were built in 1934 by the Civilian Conservation Corps, and remarkably Teton Crest remains in excellent shape after almost a century of use. In a park that receives almost four million visitors per year, the trail never feels overwhelmingly crowded either, because anyone who camps overnight in the park needs to purchase a backcountry permit in advance, which keeps numbers in check and helps distribute campsite use.

The trail officially begins at Phillips Pass, ends at String Lake, and is almost entirely within Grand Teton National Park, staying at roughly 9,000 feet of elevation most of the way. To shave off about four miles and 2,400 feet from the initial climb, however, many hikers start the trek by taking the Jackson Hole Aerial Tram from Teton Village to 10,450 feet. From the start, hikers step into an alternate universe of crazy geology—canyons, craggy peaks, glacial lakes, glaciers, and wildflower-strewn alpine meadows.

OPPOSITE: Hike in the shadow of Grand Teton in Cascade Canyon.

PAGES 124–125: The dramatic sunrise colors of the Teton Range are reflected in the water below.

It's impossible to overstate the beauty along this trail. At Death Canyon Shelf—a four-mile-long traverse of a narrow plateau—hikers thread the needle between a deep canyon on one side and a steep cliff on the other, with stunning views of 13,775-foot Grand Teton straight ahead. The shelf is not only a thoroughfare for hikers—grizzlies and other wildlife also use it to move through the mountains. After the shelf, the trail meanders out of the national park and into Alaska Basin, a wildflower-covered wilderness of glacial lakes, before returning to the park and 10,400-foot Hurricane Pass, where hikers will be gobsmacked by the view of the Grand Teton, which seems almost close enough to touch. "Everywhere you look," says Grange, "it's like geology on steroids."

From the high of Hurricane Pass, the trail dips into Cascade Canyon and back up the other side, ascending over the third pass and the highest point on the trail: 10,700-foot Paintbrush Divide. Then it's a descent through Paintbrush Canyon and back to reality at the String Lake trailhead.

WILDLIFE SIGHTING

Grizzly Bear 399, a 27-year-old, 400-pound icon of Grand Teton National Park was so beloved that she often had an entourage of 40 wildlife photographers at a time. In October 2024, 399 was killed by a motorist. She was the oldest documented grizzly bear to reproduce in the Greater Yellowstone Ecosystem, having mothered 18 known cubs.

WYOMING

TITCOMB BASIN

Lonely Wilderness With a Llama Assist

DISTANCE: 30.4 miles out and back **LENGTH OF TRIP:** 1 to 4 days **BEST TIME TO GO:** July to September
DIFFICULTY: Moderate to strenuous

Home to 19 of Wyoming's 20 highest peaks and some of the largest remaining glaciers in the lower 48, the uncrowded Wind River Range southeast of Grand Teton National Park is where locals from nearby gateway towns escape.

"Any adventure into the Wind River Range has the potential to start a transformation process in you," says Julia Heemstra, a Jackson-based athlete and international humanitarian worker who has spent the past 20 years exploring these lonely peaks. "You really feel like you're out there and exposed."

The trail that leads hikers into the heart of the range without having to technically summit a peak is an out-and-back route that starts near Pinedale. The immense appeal of this hike is that it strings together a seemingly endless necklace of glacial lakes, each with its own personality—some are ideal for camping, others appear at a perfect time to take a dip. The trail ends at Titcomb Basin, an amphitheater with twin lakes surrounded by jagged spires, including 13,804-foot Gannett Peak, the highest point in Wyoming.

Hikers who want to get out there but can't shoulder a heavy pack can take advantage of the nearby outfitters offering well-trained llamas that lighten the load.

OPPOSITE: Hiking Titcomb Basin requires lake crossings along slippery rocks.

PART TWO

OFF THE MAINLAND

Take in Hawaii's Nāpali Coast from a lookout on the Kalalau Trail (page 158).

ALASKA

CURRY RIDGE TO KESUGI RIDGE TRAIL

Denali Without the Bus Ride

DISTANCE: 46 miles one-way **LENGTH OF TRIP:** 3 to 4 days **BEST TIME TO GO:** June to September
DIFFICULTY: Moderate

Denali State Park, a 325,240-acre jewel on the southeastern flank of Denali National Park and Preserve, is often overlooked in favor of its stately elder sibling. But there is no better place to be for those who want clear views of snowcapped Mount McKinley and the surrounding Alaska Range, thanks to a 46-mile-long trail system that runs parallel to the mountains through the traditional homelands of the Dena'ina people.

Even better, unlike hiking in the national park, there's no need to wait for a bus. The new Curry Ridge Trail, completed in 2024, starts at K'esugi Ken Campground and climbs nearly 2,000 feet through subalpine and alpine terrain to reach the Kesugi Ridge Trail, an almost entirely above-the-tree-line path, along which Mount McKinley looms like a beacon, surrounded by lesser peaks and the Chulitna River carving a meandering ribbon in the foreground. Time it right and you'll camp under the dancing aurora borealis (best seen mid-August to mid-April).

Although this trail may provide easier access to hiking than the national park, it still traverses serious Alaska backcountry, home to moose and black and grizzly bears. Plus, rain, snow, and fog—even in the height of summer—can be disorienting on this highly exposed trail system.

OPPOSITE: **Backpackers can make camp with mountain views along the trail in Denali State Park.**

ALASKA

HARDING ICEFIELD TRAIL

A Retreating Wonder in Kenai Fjords National Park

DISTANCE: 8.2 miles out and back **LENGTH OF TRIP:** 5 to 7 hours **BEST TIME TO GO:** June to September
DIFFICULTY: Strenuous

An unfortunate reality: The world's glaciers are shrinking much more quickly than originally projected by scientists. Two-thirds will be melted out of existence by the year 2100, according to a recent study in the journal *Science*. But for now there are still places where one can experience the majesty of not one but many glaciers, moving together in a massive sheet of ice that flows like a river through a corridor of frozen, majestic peaks. One of these places is Kenai Fjords National Park.

Spread like a blanket across southern Alaska's Kenai Peninsula, the Harding Icefield connects 40 glaciers, covers 700 square miles, and is more than 1,000 feet thick. This hunk of ice is so enormous that it has the power to influence the region's wind, temperature, and pressure changes. Unlike massive ice fields in even more remote corners of the world, such as the northeast Greenland ice sheet, this one—or at least the portion known as Exit Glacier—is easy to reach for those willing to hike 3,000 vertical feet in 4.1 miles.

What was formerly known as Resurrection Glacier was renamed Exit Glacier in 1968 after four members of a 10-person expedition became the first to successfully cross the entire expanse of the Harding Icefield. They "exited" the glacier and finally hit solid ground after climbing 6,651-foot

OPPOSITE: Keep your eyes to the hilltops in Kenai Fjords National Park, and you may just spot a mountain goat or two.

PAGES 134-135: You can pitch your tent to wake up to sweeping views of the Harding Ice Field.

Truuli Peak, one of the many nunataks, or lonely peaks, that protrude like solitary sentinels from the depths of the ice field. Adventurers today have a head start on Exit Glacier because it has receded 1.5 miles over the past two centuries, a loss that is quickly accelerating. Since the early 2000s the glacier has retreated more than a half mile. Signs along the trail mark the glacier's former termini dating back to 1917.

Start the climb in the valley near the ranger station, slowly wind up through alders and cottonwoods, then hit alpine meadows covered with heather and dotted with fragile-looking but tenacious Arctic wildflowers, like dwarf fireweed, miniature dogwood, and salmonberries, a favorite feast for black bears that frequent the area. Even a short hike up the trail allows for a view of Exit Glacier's hulking terminus, but committed hikers who reach the top will be rewarded with a fleeting sight: a mystical realm of wind-whipped snow and ice interrupted by the occasional lonely peak. Soak it all in—this ice field has an end date.

CLIMATE WATCH

A study released in 2024 by researchers at Newcastle University in England found that glacier loss in the nearby 1,500-square-mile Juneau ice field, located north of Alaska's eponymous capital city, has shrunk at twice the yearly rate between 2010 and 2020 as the rate recorded between 1979 and 2010.

ALASKA

OOLAH VALLEY HIGH ROUTE

Off-Trail Adventure in Gates of the Arctic National Park and Preserve

DISTANCE: 35-mile-plus loop **LENGTH OF TRIP:** 10 days **BEST TIME TO GO:** June to August
DIFFICULTY: Moderate

Slightly smaller than Switzerland, entirely above the Arctic Circle, and deep in the heart of the Brooks Range is the nearly 8.4-million-acre roadless wilderness of Gates of the Arctic National Park and Preserve. One could spend an entire lifetime exploring here and never come close to knowing it fully.

"Most visitors don't have a reference for the size, scale, and scope of this park," says Dan Oberlatz, owner of Alaska Alpine Adventures, which has been offering trips in Gates of the Arctic for three decades. "It's so big it's almost incomprehensible."

That's the great beauty and terror of the northernmost park in the United States—it is so remote that there's not a visitors center, a road, or a trail. Anyone who enters the park must forge their own path. And people have been doing just that for more than 13,000 years, starting with small groups of savvy hunters who constructed mile-long rock-cairn fences to steer caribou into Agiak Lake in order to hunt them from their kayaks using long wooden lances tipped with razor-sharp stone spears. Their descendants, the Nunamiut people who historically migrated between the Arctic Ocean and the Brooks Range—settled in what is now the park in the 1940s. Today roughly 250 Nunamiut live in the village of Anaktuvuk Pass, which sits on a major caribou migratory pathway.

CLIMATE WATCH

According to a study released in 2024, rivers and streams in Gates of the Arctic National Park are turning bright orange and the fish are disappearing. What was once clean, clear blue water is now the color of rust, the result of deadly toxic metals released by thawing permafrost.

OPPOSITE: Time your hike right and you may see the aurora borealis dancing above the Brooks Range.

PAGES 138-139: Mind your step as you cross Aiyagonahala Creek.

Famously hard to reach, the park has just 11,000 annual visitors. But visitation is growing thanks to its increasingly coveted attributes of solace and a sense of freedom that hasn't changed since famed forester, author, and conservationist Bob Marshall explored the central Brooks Range back in the 1930s.

The ways to see the park are endless and may include exploring the tundra below the serrated granite edges of the Arrigetch Peaks, rafting one of six designated wild and scenic rivers, or flying over the Western Arctic caribou herd, the largest in Alaska, as they migrate north in the summer. For those who want to keep their feet firmly planted on the ground, one spectacular trail that stays in the sweet zone of alpine tundra—above the lowland scrub and bugs—is the Oolah Valley High Route.

This hike starts with a seaplane drop-off at one high-alpine lake and follows the spine of the Continental Divide, with towering peaks above and glacial carved valleys below. With layover days to explore the terrain, the trip offers the opportunity to see classic Alaska

CULTURAL HIGHLIGHT

Perched at 2,500 feet and dwarfed by surrounding mountains, the village of Anaktuvuk Pass is the only sign of civilization within the park. Connected to no outside roads, the village is self-contained, with a grocery store, museum, post office, and health clinic that's open to non-tribal members only in an emergency.

ABOVE: Gates of the Arctic National Park and Preserve is home to red foxes, along with larger wildlife.

OPPOSITE: The tundra landscape, dotted by poplars, turns marigold come fall.

megafauna, from moose and brown bears to Dall sheep and the occasional wolf. The animals are certainly out there, but the landscape here is so vast that even a herd of 15,000 caribou can disappear into it. What never disappears in the summer, however, is the endless amount and quality of daylight.

Seasoned backpackers may attempt a trip like this on their own, but there are three practical reasons to book a guide like Oberlatz: First, an experienced outfitter knows how to navigate the mountain of confounding logistics. Second, tour operators get first dibs on the increasingly in-demand flight options into the park. And finally, they have access to 24-hour satellite cell service and can arrange an emergency evacuation as quickly as humanly possible—added assurance so that hikers turn their worries off and simply enjoy this epic, once-in-a-lifetime journey.

ALASKA

DEER MOUNTAIN TRAIL

A Backyard Alaska Epic

DISTANCE: 5 miles out and back **LENGTH OF TRIP:** 4 hours **BEST TIME TO GO:** June to September **DIFFICULTY:** Strenuous

It may be just another backyard hike for resident Ketchikanians, but don't let the Deer Mountain Trail's accessibility fool you. This is an ambitious switchbacking traverse through spruce and hemlock in Tongass National Forest and up, up, up to the summit of Deer Mountain, which looms like a sleeping giant over the city (with a population just over 8,000). Because the trailhead is so close to Ketchikan and can be accomplished in just a few hours, it's a also tantalizing hike for cruisers making their way along the southeast Alaska coastline. But get those sea legs firmly underfoot before attempting it: The trail climbs almost 3,000 feet in just 2.5 miles, often in wet, slippery conditions and through prime black bear habitat.

The first jaw-dropping view is a mile up and looks out over Revillagigedo Island and across the Tongass Narrows to Pennock, Gravina, and Annett Islands. It's worth it to press on toward the summit, because the terrain turns to alpine meadows, and the panorama gets only more expansive with every step. At one point there's mountainous Ketchikan Lake below and vistas toward the Dude and Diana Mountains. At another, there's the endless Pacific Ocean. After the final push to the summit, the entire coastline unfurls to the southeast all the way to the white-capped peaks of British Columbia.

OPPOSITE: The steep route ascending Deer Mountain is surrounded by picturesque forest.

ALASKA AND CANADA

CHILKOOT TRAIL

A Gold Rush in the Klondike

DISTANCE: 33 miles one-way **LENGTH OF TRIP:** 3 to 5 days **BEST TIME TO GO:** June to mid-September
DIFFICULTY: Strenuous

In August 1896 a Tlingit and Tagish man named Keish (who went down in history as Skookum Jim Mason) discovered gold on Rabbit Creek, a tributary of the Klondike River. But it was his expedition mate, American George Carmack, who staked the claim that sparked the Klondike gold rush. Within a year, a tsunami of people set out for the Klondike in search of riches.

To reach this region of the remote Yukon Territory in northwestern Canada, most miners took the least expensive and most direct of several routes: sailing from Seattle up the Inside Passage and disembarking in Skagway, Alaska, then traveling a mostly dirt road 25 minutes to Dyea to reach the start of the Chilkoot Trail. By the winter of 1897–98, Dyea, formerly an isolated seasonal fishing camp for the Chilkat Tlingit people, had become a boomtown, with two newspapers, a telephone company, and multiple saloons.

From Dyea, stampeders set out on the trail, trudging 3,500 feet up and over Chilkoot Pass to Lake Bennett, where they built boats at the headwaters of the Yukon River and sailed to Dawson City. This path to gold, however, had its hazards—both human and natural. There were murders, robberies, diseases, and death by malnutrition. But the biggest catastrophe of all hit on Palm Sunday in 1898 when a deadly avalanche let loose just north of Sheep Camp, almost halfway up the trail. Indigenous peoples who were veterans of the trail knew better than to climb above the high-alpine terrain of Sheep Camp, but some stampeders ignored their

OPPOSITE: The Chilkoot Trail passes through the forests of Klondike Gold Rush National Historical Park.

PAGES 146-147: White Pass sits on the border of Alaska and British Columbia, Canada.

warnings. It smothered hundreds and killed more than 70 stampeders, some of whom were buried in up to 50 feet of snow.

Today the Chilkoot Trail is a popular recreational path for day hikers and backpackers, with nine established camping areas along the route. Littered with remnants of the gold rush, from broken-down pianos to castaway books to the rusted remains of the Scales (a tramway system that moved goods over the pass), it's a surreal step into the past.

Modern conveniences like satellite communications make the hike less dangerous, but there are still hazards. In 2022, the same year it was officially designated a national historic trail, the Chilkoot sustained major flood damage that destroyed bridges, campsites, and other amenities. It is slowly reopening but hikers need to be hyperaware that this trail—which starts in a coastal forest in Alaska, ascends into high-alpine tundra, and descends back into a boreal forest in British Columbia—is a serious and remote undertaking. Be aware: An emergency evacuation can cost upwards of $75,000.

KNOW BEFORE YOU GO

To reserve an overnight camping permit on the trail, even hikers starting on the U.S. side must call Parks Canada's Chilkoot Reservation Line (800-661-0486). The trail is so popular that Parks Canada receives hundreds of calls in the first hour that reservations open. Leave a message; they *will* call back.

Summit

Even in the summer, portions of the Chilkoot are prone to avalanche. It also rains almost every day, which means slogging through rushing creeks or hiking through dense fog in the high country, which can be very disorienting when scrambling over an unmarked route that consists of little more than a scree field. This is also the home to black *and* brown bears.

But for those who come prepared—and have made the proper advance camping reservations by calling (not emailing) Parks Canada—the trail offers an international wilderness experience like no other. Chilkoot has acute reminders of a chaotic and exciting moment in history around every corner mixed with complete stretches of utter solitude. When hikers finally arrive at Lake Bennett, they can hop a train or a floatplane out.

ABOVE: **You'll need to be comfortable with a little bit of scrambling to ascend the Golden Stairs in Chilkoot Pass.**

OPPOSITE: **Find respite in a cabin at the top of Chilkoot Pass.**

AMERICAN SAMOA

MOUNT ALAVA ADVENTURE TRAIL

Traveling Through Time on Sacred Earth

DISTANCE: 5.6-mile loop **LENGTH OF TRIP:** 4 hours **BEST TIME TO GO:** December to April
DIFFICULTY: Strenuous

For hikers on a quest to knock off all 63 national parks, one of the last they will likely reach is the National Park of American Samoa. Samoa, whose name means "sacred earth," is a tropical oasis of seven volcanic islands and atolls in the South Pacific and has the only national park south of the Equator. The park is scattered across four of the islands: Tutuila, Ta'ū, Ofu, and Olosega, all of which are ringed by coral-sand beaches and home to a riot of birdlife, including the endemic day-flying fruit bat, which has a sprawling three-foot wingspan.

Unlike every other national park, the U.S. government does not own the National Park of American Samoa outright. In 1993 the federal government entered into a land-lease agreement with the Samoans, who are descendants of Polynesia's oldest culture, which dates back 3,000 years to when the islands' first inhabitants arrived from Asia. Thanks to this visionary arrangement, Samoans' way of life, known as *fa'asamoa,* has been beautifully preserved, including communal land ownership and a daily village-wide time for prayer known as *sa*. Because there is little in the way of tourism infrastructure and no camping is allowed, guests can fully embrace *fa'asamoa* during a homestay. The first rule: Always ask permission, even to do an activity as benign as taking a swim. Beaches are communally owned (not public), and swimming is forbidden on Sundays.

OPPOSITE: **Birders will love looking to the skies along the Mount Alava Adventure Trail for species such as the collared kingfisher.**

PAGES 152-153: **Samoan culture thrives in Aüa village, which sits below Rainmaker Mountain on Tutuila.**

Asking for permission is not only polite but also a wise way to quickly learn about lurking dangers, which extend to hiking the lush interior of the islands, where muddy trails and aging infrastructure can pose extreme risks to hikers. This is especially true on Tutuila's Mount Alava Adventure Trail, a steep route that begins east of the village of Vatia and across from a trailhead of the Lower Sauma Ridge Trail (which goes in the opposite direction toward the coastline). Mount Alava Adventure Trail's overgrown path climbs sharply through a tropical rainforest teeming with fruit bats and birds and is equipped with slippery wooden ladders and ropes to help hikers navigate precipitous sections. At last count there were 56 ladders and 783 steps.

Hikers then follow Maugaloa Ridge to the summit of 1,610-foot Mount Alava, the highest point in the park. Most of the hike is through such dense tropical foliage that, despite the height of the ridgeline, it's hard to see much. At the summit, however, the scene opens to the cerulean Pacific and the serrated edges of Matafao Peak in the distance.

CULTURAL HIGHLIGHT

There are no cabins in the park, and camping is not permitted. Instead, hikers can lodge at a traditional Samoan *fale,* a domed, thatch-roofed hut, where guests join their hosts in village activities such as cutting pandanus leaves to dry for weaving mats and eat meals like *oka,* raw fish marinated in coconut cream, lemon juice, chili, and onions.

GUAM

SELLA BAY TO CETTI FALLS LOOP

A North Pacific Idyll

DISTANCE: 5.5-mile loop **LENGTH OF TRIP:** 4 hours **BEST TIME TO GO:** January to June
DIFFICULTY: Strenuous

The U.S. territory of Guam, a land of swaying palms and white sand beaches, is the southernmost island in the Northern Marianas chain and sits 5,800 miles west of San Francisco. For being a 250-square-mile dot in the North Pacific, it has played an outsize role in history.

Guam's first residents, the CHamoru, arrived at least 2,000 years ago from islands off Southeast Asia. In 1521, explorer Ferdinand Magellan was the first known European to set foot on Guam. Thirty years later, Spain officially declared the island its own and it became a major stop for galleons traveling between Acapulco and the Philippines. At the end of the Spanish American War, Spain ceded the island to the United States. Save for a cruel, 2.5-year rule by Japan during World War II, during which hundreds of CHamoru were enslaved, tortured, or executed, Guam has been a U.S. territory ever since. To some Americans, the island's strong military presence can overshadow its natural beauty.

"Guam's outstanding hiking destinations to beaches, caves, historic sites, and waterfalls are too often hidden beneath the appearance of the island just being a military base," says Dave Lotz, the first president of the Guam Boonie Stompers, a decades-old hiking organization.

One of the island's most rewarding hikes is a loop on its southern end.

OPPOSITE: Sunsets over Sella Bay are majestic.

PAGES 156-157: The jungle landscape has reclaimed the Spanish Bridge at Sella Bay.

It starts at the Sella Bay trailhead on Route 2 between the villages of Hågat and Humåtak and descends through rolling hills covered in tropical forests and grasslands, crossing two streams to Sella Bay. Near the Pacific coastline hikers will pass the remains of the double-arch, cut-stone Spanish Bridge and what's left of El Camino Real, a Spanish-colonial-era road that started in the port of Humåtak and ended in the colonial capital of Hagåtña. Near the bridge are ruins of a Spanish beehive oven and latte stones, top-heavy pillars used by the CHamoru to build their homes.

At the beach, hikers can take a cooling dip and walk south along the shoreline around a volcanic pillar to Cetti Bay, a crescent-moon-shaped inlet lined with coconut palms. From Cetti Bay, the hike back up to Route 2 requires wading through a stream to a natural pool at the base of the first of seven waterfalls, which hikers climb using ropes. At the top of the last waterfall, hikers have a stunning view of the verdant valley, the cerulean water, and, if timed right, the sun setting over the Philippine Sea.

HISTORICAL FOOTNOTE

When in Guam, take time to stop at War in the Pacific National Historical Park, the only park in the system that honors the bravery and sacrifice of *all* soldiers who served in the Pacific theater during World War II, including Americans, the Allied nations, and the Japanese.

HAWAII

KALALAU TRAIL

The North Pacific of the Past

DISTANCE: 22 miles out and back **LENGTH OF TRIP:** 1 to 6 days **BEST TIME TO GO:** Late spring and summer
DIFFICULTY: Strenuous

The storied Kalalau Trail on the island of Kauai offers a portal into a tropical Pacific of the past. The path bisects fluted emerald peaks that drop hundreds of feet into the crashing surf. There's potential for rock falls, flash floods, and fierce winds, but the exposure to raw wilderness and the trail's Edenic beauty are what make it so exhilarating.

The coastline began to form millions of years ago when magma from multiple volcanic eruptions cooled. The serrated ridges that make the Nāpali Coast so singular are the result of water erosional forces emanating from the wettest environment on Earth at the top, combined with the power of the crashing ocean waves at the bottom. The result for hikers is a trail that climbs into and out of five steep valleys, requiring 2,500 feet of ascent before ending at half-mile-long Kalalau Beach. There hikers can pitch a tent above the sand, fall asleep to the sound of crashing waves, or hike two miles inland to a traditional terraced taro field now overgrown with introduced java plum, guava, and mango trees.

This seemingly uninhabitable coastline was occupied for an estimated millennium by Hawaiians who farmed taro, fished in the Pacific, and built temples and shrines to their deities. These Indigenous peoples were completely isolated until what is now the Kalalau Trail was built in the 1860s. Evidence of the former inhabitants exists in the remnants of irrigation ditches, terraced fields, house platforms, temples, shrines, and graves. These ruins are almost invisible to the untrained eye because they

KNOW BEFORE YOU GO

Day hikers are allowed to trek two miles to Hanakapiʻai Beach but need to buy an advance entry pass to Hāʻena State Park and a parking or shuttle pass online at *gohaena.com*. Overnight campers can apply for the required permit up to 90 days in advance at *dlnr.hawaii.gov*.

OPPOSITE: The fluted ridges of the Nāpali Coast rise above the crashing surf on Kauai's north shore.

PAGES 160-161: Look out over Hanakapiʻai Beach from the Kalalau Trail.

were built to blend seamlessly into the landscape, and today relentless erosion continues to degrade them.

Until recently, up to 3,000 hikers a day set out to experience the magic of the Nāpali Coast. With the crowds came the usual pitfalls: illegal camping, destruction of historic sites, and occasional fatalities. The most hardcore of these hikers were squatters who would live illegally at Kalalau for months at a time, destroying rock walls built by Native Hawaiians to build their own structures and living off wild avocados and whatever else they could barter with visiting boaters or backpackers.

For decades Hawaii's Department of Land and Natural Resources (DLNR) worked in conjunction with Kauai's North Shore community to implement new policies within Hā'ena State Park—the gateway to Nāpali's 6,175 acres of majestic wilderness—that would mitigate the cultural and environmental damage that came with overuse. In 2018, opportunity arose in the aftermath of a massive storm that struck Kauai's North Shore, dropping a record-breaking

CULTURAL HIGHLIGHT

Those with a valid Hawaii hunting license and hunter education card are allowed to bow-hunt feral pigs and goats along the trail. The best pig hunting is in the first six miles. For goats, it's between miles six and 11. If successful, be prepared for a long hike out carrying your kill.

ABOVE: Hike among the lush greenery on trails that lead to ocean views.

OPPOSITE: Though some waterfalls are easier to reach, Hanakapi'ai Falls takes a challenging eight-mile round-trip trek.

50 inches of rain in 24 hours, closing Hāʻena State Park and neighboring Nāpali Coast State Wilderness Park for almost a year. During the cleanup, officials rebuilt park infrastructure and instituted a permit and entry-pass system that limits visitors to 900 a day. Today, about 150,000 visitors make their way to the park annually.

A successful piece of the new plan is a reservation-only shuttle system that runs between the resort town of Princeville and Hāʻena State Park. Park a car illegally on the side of the road near the park entrance and be prepared to receive a $200 ticket. When conditions are too dangerous to hike, the shuttle stops running. "We have deliberately created a system that doesn't allow everybody who wants to go, to go," says Alan Carpenter, assistant administrator at the DLNR Division of State Parks. "The difficulty of you getting into the park is what is saving it."

HAWAII

KEONEHE'EHE'E AND HALEMAU'U TRAILS

Chasing the Sun in Haleakalā National Park

DISTANCE: 11.2 miles one-way **LENGTH OF TRIP:** 6 to 8 hours **BEST TIME TO GO:** May to October
DIFFICULTY: Strenuous

The antithesis of a laid-back Hawaiian beach vacation, a hike through the heart of the Summit District in Maui's Haleakalā National Park feels more like trekking on the moon. Temperatures near the summit of the park are roughly 20 degrees colder than they are at sea level and often drop below freezing; afternoon thunderstorms can roll through, leaving unsuspecting hikers drenched; and at this elevation, there's always the threat of altitude sickness.

It's worth the potential discomfort to experience Haleakalā, or "house of the sun," one of the most important spiritual centers in Hawaii. This dormant shield volcano is part of *wao akua,* or the "realm of the gods." Since the first peoples arrived on Maui from their ancient homeland, they have used the 10,023-foot summit of Haleakalā as a place of pilgrimage, ceremony, and intentional resource extraction.

The volcano last erupted between 1480 and 1600, and it may very well erupt again. But what is now deemed the "crater" is really a large erosional depression carved over millennia by wind and rain. Subsequent eruptions filled the valley with black lava beds and *pu'u* (red cinder cones), turning it into an alien landscape sprouting with *'āhinahina,* or Mauna Loa silversword,

OPPOSITE: Hōlua Campground is nestled in the crater's backcountry among tall cliffs. You'll find clear night skies here thanks to the very low light pollution.

PAGES 166-167: You'll feel like you're hiking on another planet in the landscapes of Haleakalā.

MSR

a yucca-like plant that can take up to a half century to flower. It sends up a spectacular stalk with a blood-red blossom and dies soon afterward, scattering its seeds to the wind.

One of the best ways to explore the crater is to drop from the rim at the Keonehe'ehe'e (Sliding Sands) trailhead, cross the valley floor almost four miles, and then hike back up the other side on the Halemau'u Trail. Roughly halfway into the hike, after turning northeast onto the Halemau'u Trail, hikers will find Pele's Paint Pot on the north side of the Halāli'i cinder cone. Along this technicolor passage you'll feel as if you're walking over a rainbow that melted into the landscape. Nearby is Kawilinau, once known as the "bottomless pit," a fenced-off black hole about 65 feet deep that, according to legend, descends to the ocean.

Many Hawaiian *mo'olelo,* or stories, reference Haleakalā. One tells of how the demigod Māui, dismayed by the short days, climbed Haleakalā and snared the sun with cords from his elders. Slowing down the sun, he gave his mother more time to dry her *kapa,* the traditional cloth made from the bark of the wauke plant.

KNOW BEFORE YOU GO

Watching the sun rise from Haleakalā is worth the predawn wakeup. There are four premier viewing locations, but reservations are required to access the park between 3 and 7 a.m. Book a reservation through *recreation.gov* or with one of a handful of approved tour companies on the National Park Service website.

HAWAII

MAKAPU'U POINT LIGHTHOUSE TRAIL

Where the Whales Are

DISTANCE: 2.5 miles out and back **LENGTH OF TRIP:** 1 to 2 hours **BEST TIME TO GO:** Year-round
DIFFICULTY: Easy

At the southeasternmost tip of Oahu, six miles east of Honolulu and within Kaiwi State Scenic Shoreline, this 500-foot uphill hike offers an easy summit for the entire family. It also boasts sensational views. To the southwest are the twin volcanic tuff cones of Koko Head and Koko Crater; just offshore are rocky islets alive with the cacophony of Hawaiian seabirds; and straight out in the Pacific lies the chance to see humpback whales migrating from Alaska between November and May. As many as 10,000 whales come every year to mate, give birth, and nurse their calves.

The prize—just below the end of the trail and sitting atop a rocky, solitary cliff—is a historic, red-roofed lighthouse. Built in 1909, the station is still used by the U.S. Coast Guard, so it's off-limits to the public. But even from a distance, visitors can see the original 12-foot-tall Fresnel lens, which reflects rays of light from more than 1,000 prisms. It was designed by famed French physicist Augustin-Jean Fresnel and to this day remains the largest lighthouse lens in use by the United States, with a range of 19 nautical miles. Reminiscent of a giant, translucent Easter egg, it dwarfs its keepers.

OPPOSITE: **Makapu'u Point Lighthouse was built in 1909 and is still in use by the U.S. Coast Guard.**

NORTHERN MARIANA ISLANDS

FORBIDDEN ISLAND

A Legendary Hike With a Cautionary Tale

DISTANCE: 2 miles out and back **LENGTH OF TRIP:** 2 hours **BEST TIME TO GO:** April to July
DIFFICULTY: Moderate

Arcing like a crescent-moon constellation in the North Pacific Ocean, the 14 islands of the Northern Mariana Archipelago have a total land mass of 183.5 square miles. Ten of these islands are largely uninhabited and small, without much room for a lengthy thru-hike. What the southernmost Northern Marianas have in abundance, however, is dramatic tropical beauty, with coconuts and papayas growing wild, slivers of white sand beaches, and limestone cliffs dropping into the sea.

One of the most beloved hikes is on Saipan—the largest of the Mariana Islands and capital of the Northern Marianas—to a close-up view of Forbidden Island, a flat-topped rock outcropping that juts off the Kagman Peninsula on the island's eastern coastline. The hike begins high on a cliff that rises more than 300 feet straight up from the Western Pacific waves crashing along rugged Unai Hakmaing beach. On top, the trail is thick with tangantangan, a wispy, fernlike castor-oil plant. The descent, which is steep in places, leads to the beach and a small area of protected tide pools teeming with marine life. At low tide, a string of rocks stretch to Forbidden Island, but don't be tempted to cross. The water here is ferocious, as attested to by a marker memorializing four Boy Scouts who were tragically hit by a rogue wave here and swept out to sea on February 18, 1973.

OPPOSITE: Hike your way to the Forbidden Island.

PUERTO RICO

CAÑÓN SAN CRISTÓBAL

The Comeback Canyon

DISTANCE: 4 miles out and back **LENGTH OF TRIP:** 4 to 6 hours **BEST TIME TO GO:** December to June
DIFFICULTY: Strenuous

In the lush heart of Puerto Rico lies a canyon that was undisturbed by humans until the 19th century. Named after St. Christopher, the third-century patron saint of travelers, Cañón San Cristóbal plunges dramatically, roughly 700 feet in less than a mile. With near-vertical canyon walls for the first half mile, it widens to a steep-sided river valley through which the Río Usabón and several smaller tributaries flow.

But it's only recently that humans have been able to enjoy the spectacular diversity and beauty of this canyon. Throughout the 19th and early 20th centuries, the surrounding forest was cleared for pastures and fields and the canyon became a garbage dump into which heavy metal machinery and all manner of refuse were thrown. In the 1960s conservationists started a campaign to protect the area. In 1972 the Conservation Trust of Puerto Rico bought its first tract of land within the canyon, and the landfill was finally closed in 1974. But it wasn't until 2013 that Puerto Rico officially declared 6,881 acres of the canyon a protected natural area.

Today, life in Cañón San Cristóbal is bouncing back and holds an exciting variety of flora that thrives in an annual average rainfall of nearly 60 inches. In a 1998 survey, the International Institute of Tropical Forestry counted 677 species of plants, from common evergreen shrubs to rare tree species that predate colonization. Another survey found 695 species of birds, from

OPPOSITE: Take in the beauty of Cristóbal Falls from the trail.

PAGES 174-175: Not just sand and sea, this hike explores the mountain and valley greenery of Puerto Rico.

mangrove cuckoos to peregrine falcons, and 144 species of animals, such as the Puerto Rican ground lizard.

It's a stunning success story after nearly a century of degradation. Rusted old machinery from the landfill can still be seen in places, but a hike into this canyon—one of the most dramatic features on the island—presents a rare opportunity to experience a lost world. The precipitous hike quickly drops hundreds of feet to the canyon floor near the base of 230-foot La Niebla. One of the highest waterfalls in Puerto Rico, it cascades off sheer walls of hard black lava.

The hike farther downstream offers an adventure over hard-pack trail and scrambling along the riverbed to more stunning cascades, like 30-foot-tall Salto de la Cabra, and deep, refreshing swimming holes like Charco Azul. To go any farther requires rappelling down wet rock while being doused from above by water, which sounds like a perfect hike in a climate where the average annual temperature is 70°F.

THE CHALLENGE

In August 2024, while the island was still recovering from the ferocity of Hurricane Maria, which roared through in 2017, Hurricane Ernesto dropped heavy rains. Some national forests, like El Yunque, were closed indefinitely after Ernesto, so it's wise to time your visit before August or after November to avoid hurricane season.

U.S. VIRGIN ISLANDS

REEF BAY TRAIL

A Hike Through Historical Complexities

DISTANCE: 5 miles out and back **LENGTH OF TRIP:** 4 hours **BEST TIME TO GO:** November to May
DIFFICULTY: Moderate

The layers of St. John island's history lie in plain view along the Reef Bay Trail, which starts at 800 feet of elevation at a trailhead off Centerline Road. The path passes an amalgamation of historic sites that date back thousands of years. But it's not only the fascinating history that makes this one of the most popular hikes in Virgin Islands National Park. It's also that hikers get summit views of St. Croix and the shimmering Caribbean right from the start, followed by a descent into the deep shade of tropical forest dotted with brilliant West Indian locust, mango, and kapok trees, and then a swim at Reef Bay Beach at the end.

Roughly halfway down the trail, a spur to the right takes hikers two-tenths of a mile to one of the most important sites on the island: an amphitheater with a freshwater pool that is primed by a cascading waterfall during the late autumn rainy season. Just above the high-water mark is a series of Indigenous rock art that is believed to have been carved by the Taino people, who inhabited St. John in the pre-Columbian era.

There is endless speculation as to what these figures represent, but most experts agree that the small faces with outsize, hollow eyes gazing back at the viewer are remembrances of dead ancestors or depictions of beings in the supernatural world—or both. The position of the art just

POST-HIKE ACTIVITY

There's only one good way to cool off after an epic hike through a dry tropical forest: swim! Accessible only by hiking or boat, Reef Bay Beach is luxuriously isolated on the island's south shore. There is good snorkeling in the bay, but beware of rough water on the south side of the bay.

OPPOSITE: Take a break from the trail to enjoy the sand and waves at Reef Bay.

PAGES 178-179: Park rangers lead hikes and offer insight into the island's flora and fauna.

above the waterline allows for a mirror image reflected in the pool that speaks to their spooky duality. "It's a magical place. There's an energy to it," says Mark Gestwicki, program director for Friends of Virgin Islands National Park, the non-profit organization that maintains the park's trails. "The artwork really makes you wonder what the people were trying to get across."

Several other historic sites are accessible from the trail, including the crumbling foundations of four sugar estates. These tell the story of Dutch colonization, which began in 1717 when the fields of nearby St. Thomas began to wear thin. Within a decade, all useful agricultural land on St. John was taken. Sugar factories, slave villages, and estate houses such as the Reef Bay Estate Great House—which can be seen on the hike, now overgrown with rainforest vines—fanned out across the island.

Near the end of the trail is the crumbling brick facade of the Reef Bay sugar mill and the remains of its steam-powered machinery. First used as a cattle and cotton plantation in the 18th century, the building was repurposed to

HISTORICAL FOOTNOTE

St. John is filled with reminders of how this peaceful haven was once part of the brutal trans-Atlantic slave trade. Annaberg Plantation, one of 25 sugar plantations on the island in 1780, used hundreds of enslaved laborers to clear land, terrace hillsides, and work over boiling kettles of cane juice to produce sugar.

ABOVE: **Look for Taino petroglyphs along the hiking trail.**

OPPOSITE: **You can explore the ruins of the Reef Bay Estate Great House along the trail.**

process sugarcane into sugar and for distilling rum, until production stopped abruptly following a fatal accident in 1908. Afterward, the land was turned back over to cattle raising. In another horrific turn of events, Anna Marsh, the daughter of estate owner William H. Marsh, an Englishman from nearby Tortola, was murdered in the house next to the factory in 1941. Today, hikers can walk the grounds of the factory on their own or take a guided tour to learn more about its history on the island.

The island's dark past stands in stark contrast to the surrounding beauty. Hikers can mull it all over during a cooling swim off Reef Bay Beach, an empty stretch of yellow sand at the trail's end. For those uninterested in the steep and sweaty uphill trek back out, the park offers a twice-weekly guided ranger hike that ends with a boat ride from the beach back to Cruz Bay.

PART THREE

THE EAST & THE MID-ATLANTIC

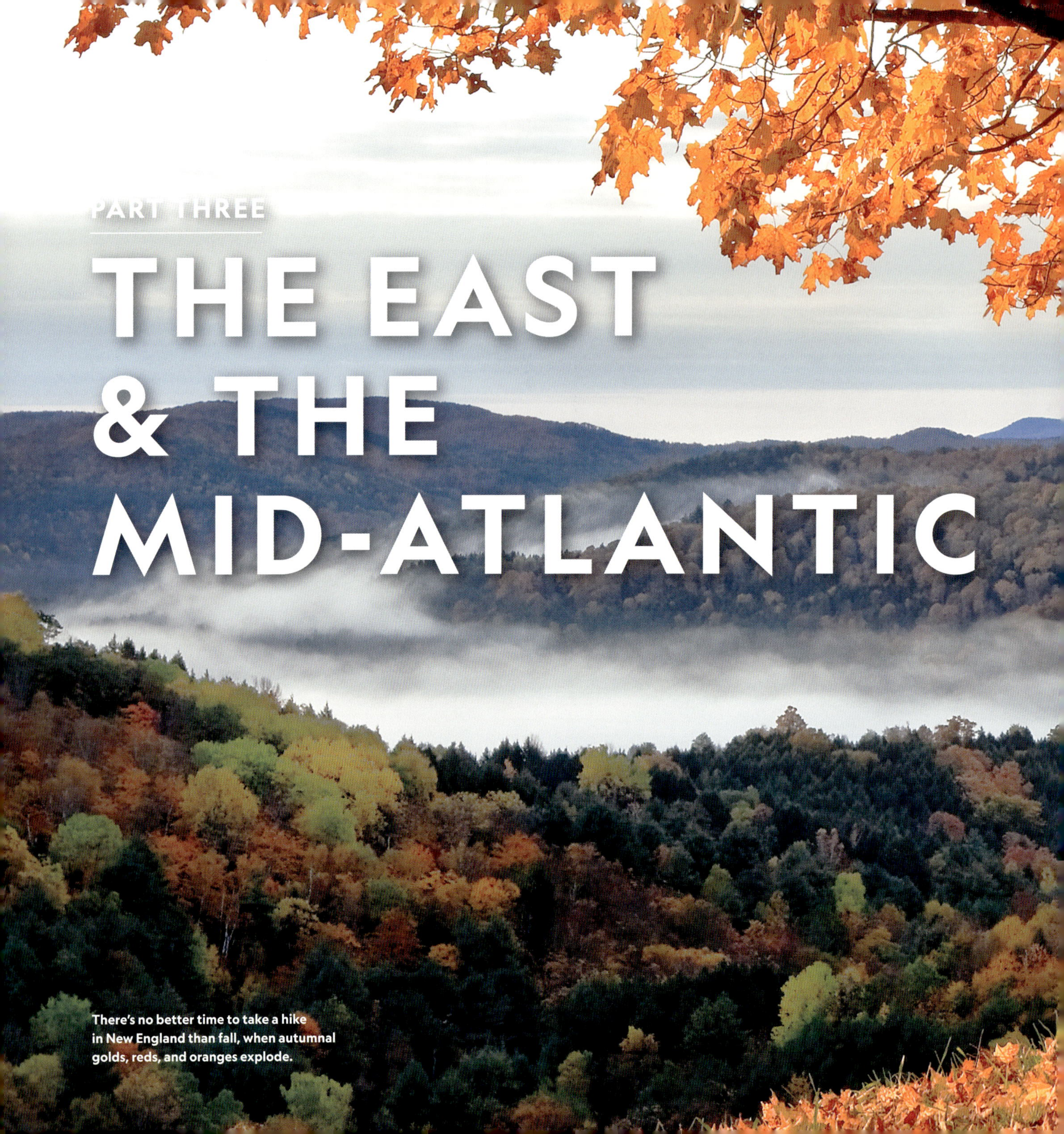

There's no better time to take a hike in New England than fall, when autumnal golds, reds, and oranges explode.

CONNECTICUT

METACOMET TRAIL

Where Cultures Clashed

DISTANCE: 62.3 miles one-way **LENGTH OF TRIP:** 3 to 4 days **BEST TIME TO GO:** May to October
DIFFICULTY: Moderate

Part of the 235-mile New England National Scenic Trail (page 208), the Metacomet is a south-to-north shot through the center of Connecticut that veers just west of Hartford and follows the trap rock ridgelines that rise 500 feet above pastoral farms, historic villages, and encroaching development.

Named after the 17th-century Wampanoag chief Metacom, the trail holds space for an important turning point in U.S. history. Metacom, also known as King Philip, clashed with colonists over diminishing resources and wary alliances, which led to the nearly three-year-long First Indian War. It ended tragically for Metacom, whose severed head was mounted on a pike near the entrance to Plymouth, Massachusetts, for more than two decades.

The trail offers no such grisly reminders, but there are multiple historic sites from Metacom's time interspersed with bucolic New England beauty and leafy deciduous forests that flame red and gold in autumn. There are also tricky sections along Metacomet Ridge that require clamoring up and over the volcanic basalt and sedimentary rock tilted in precarious positions to reach high points like 750-foot Rattlesnake Mountain and Heublein Tower, a historic residence in what is now Talcott Mountain State Park. With a viewing shed oriented toward the west, the sunsets from precipitous Metacomet Ridge are divine.

OPPOSITE: Snowshoes help winter hikers enjoy a trek across Mount Holyoke for Connecticut River Valley views.

DELAWARE

GORDONS POND TRAIL

An Avian Superhighway

DISTANCE: 6.4 miles out and back **LENGTH OF TRIP:** 3 hours **BEST TIME TO GO:** Spring to fall
DIFFICULTY: Easy

Cape Henlopen juts into the water like a giant comma where Delaware Bay and the Atlantic Ocean meet. In 1682 William Penn, the founder of Pennsylvania and Delaware, declared this stunning windswept strip of shifting sand public land, allowing the residents to fish, harvest oysters, and gather plums, cranberries, and huckleberries.

Since colonial times Cape Henlopen has played a strategic role in defending cities upriver, like Wilmington and Philadelphia, from attack. During World War II more than 2,300 U.S. Army soldiers were stationed here in a small military city known as Fort Miles. It had 16 underground bunkers, including the 15,000-square-foot Battery 519, an artillery emplacement that now houses a museum where visitors can learn about the base's critical role in World War II and later the Cold War, as a top-secret U.S. Navy listening post. From Fort Miles, the U.S. Navy unfurled a cable 104 miles into the Atlantic that was equipped with 40 underwater microphones strong enough to detect and determine Russian submarine positions.

In 1964 the U.S. Department of Defense declared 543 acres of Cape Henlopen as surplus property, and Delaware created Cape Henlopen State Park. What had once been a top-secret military base stocked with munitions became a playground of mature maritime forests, saltwater lagoons, and windswept beaches—a wild oasis for humans and animals alike.

OPPOSITE: Ring-billed gulls wade in the waters of Gordons Pond in Cape Henlopen State Park.

PAGES 188-189: Along the trail, find pathways to the Delaware seaside and its sandy shores.

Just south of the Fort Miles Historical Area, between the Lewes and Rehoboth Canal and the Atlantic Ocean, is the Gordons Pond Trail, a flat thoroughfare of crushed rock that connects the resort towns of Lewes in the north to Rehoboth Beach in the south. An easy stroll for all ages, and accessible to wheelchairs with all-terrain tires, the trail skirts Gordons Pond, a 900-acre saltwater lagoon. This is one of the best places along the Atlantic flyway to slow down and listen to the glorious sounds of migrating waterfowl, including sea ducks, loons, and gannets in the fall and early spring; herons, egrets, and ibises in the summer; and hawks in the fall.

Running parallel to the trail is a long, stunning, sandy coastline, the highest point of which is the Great Dune, the largest sand hill between Cape Cod, Massachusetts, and Cape Hatteras, North Carolina. This big pile of sand, which towers 64 feet above sea level, has been used over the centuries as a grandstand to watch activity in the ocean, from marauding pirates to invading British during the War of 1812.

WILDLIFE SIGHTING

The Cornell Lab of Ornithology's eBird, the comprehensive web-based tool for recording bird observations, lists Cape Henlopen State Park as a "birding hot spot" with 321 recorded species, from short-eared owls to orange-crowned warblers to dickcissels. Gordons Pond within the park is on one of only four North American "migration superhighways" for waterfowl.

GEORGIA TO MAINE

APPALACHIAN TRAIL

America's Most Iconic Thru-Hike

DISTANCE: 2,197 miles one-way **LENGTH OF TRIP:** 5 to 7 months **BEST TIME TO GO:** Late spring to early fall
DIFFICULTY: Strenuous

As American as apple pie and the Fourth of July, the Appalachian Trail (AT), which winds 2,197 miles through 13 states from Georgia to Maine, is the original epic thru-hike. Almost a century old, the well-established trail offers sections of remote solitude, extreme physical challenge, and deeply rooted community support throughout one of the most densely populated regions of the country.

For most thru-hikers the trail begins at the 3,782-foot summit of Springer Mountain in Georgia and ends at the top of 5,270-foot Mount Katahdin in Maine. Between those two points the trail undulates roughly 520,000 feet, which is about 30,000 feet more than its sibling on the West Coast, the Pacific Crest Trail (page 46). Some people take decades to complete the AT in its entirety. Others treat it as a race; Tara Dower, who currently holds the record for the trail's fastest known time, or FKT, ran and walked the trail in 40 days, 18 hours, and 6 minutes. No matter what their pace, all AT thru-hikers are wise to come prepared and heed the saying "No pain, no rain, no Maine."

The trail's endpoints have remained unchanged since it was completed in 1937. What has changed, however, is the nature and distance of the trail itself. In September 2024, fueled by exceedingly warm waters in the Gulf of Mexico, Hurricane Helene tore a path through the Appalachians in the worst natural disaster the trail has ever experienced, especially in North Carolina,

HISTORICAL FOOTNOTE

In 1921, Harvard-educated forester Benton MacKaye wrote "An Appalachian Trail, a Project in Regional Planning." Sixteen years later, with a whole lot of hard work from the Civilian Conservation Corps and others, MacKaye's dream path was completed.

OPPOSITE: The portion of the Appalachian Trail in Bakersville, North Carolina, is quite family friendly.

PAGES 192–193: More than three million hikers take on at least a portion of the Appalachian Trail each year; of those, about 3,000 complete the entire thru-hike.

Tennessee, and West Virginia, where an unprecedented number of trees blew down, bridges were washed away, and portions of the trail became impassable. Worse, trail communities like Hot Springs, North Carolina, were devastated.

"Aesthetically it's going to be quite stark in some places for a long time," says Hawk Metheny, the Appalachian Trail Conservancy's vice president of trail management. The good news, though, is that the aftermath of the storm resulted in an army of volunteers coming forward to help clean up. The conservancy also established the Appalachian Trail Resiliency Fund, which will help mitigate future climate change disasters by supporting necessities like longer, higher bridges built to withstand flooding.

For hikers, "adaptation and flexibility will be the key attributes" going forward, says Metheny, adding that a point-to-point thru-hike may become increasingly difficult as sections of the trail go

BY THE NUMBERS

- **5 million:** Steps it takes to hike the entire Appalachian Trail
- **3 to 4 million:** People who hike a portion of the trail each year
- **200,000:** Volunteer hours through the Appalachian Trail Conservancy each year
- **6,000:** Active volunteers who put in those hours
- **99:** Percent of the AT that has been rebuilt or relocated since its original completion in 1937
- **83:** Age of the oldest-known person to thru-hike the trail
- **33.9 pounds:** Average thru-hiker pack weight in 2024

ABOVE: **For those who need a break from their tents, Maine offers cabin shelters along the Appalachian Trail.**

OPPOSITE: **Enjoy sunset views from Annapolis Rock on the South Mountain State Park portion of the trail in Maryland.**

offline to be rebuilt or are closed because of increased flooding or wildfires. "Doing a northbound hike starting at Springer Mountain may not be feasible," says Metheny. "So starting farther north and returning later in the year when the trail is clear—known as a flip-flop—may be more advisable."

No matter the sequence hikers travel the Appalachian Trail, they will experience its magic and glory, from sublime sunrises to alpine meadows bursting with wildflowers to trail angels lending a hand. But they will also be subject to its pain, from drenching rain to punishing, precipitous rocky climbs. The highs and lows are all a part of this life-giving path that builds strength, forges deep friendships, and takes anyone who rises to the challenge to places they never imagined they could go.

"The AT is a much cherished, much regarded resource," says Metheny. "That is what has sustained it until today, and that is what will sustain it into the future."

MAINE

MOUNT KATAHDIN LOOP

Wilderness Preservation First, Recreation Second

DISTANCE: 8.3 miles round-trip **LENGTH OF TRIP:** 8 to 12 hours **BEST TIME TO GO:** June to October
DIFFICULTY: Strenuous

As the northern terminus of the Appalachian Trail and the southern terminus of the International Appalachian Trail, 5,270-foot Mount Katahdin is a coveted peak to summit. It wasn't always this way. The Penobscot people, whose traditional lands include the tallest peak in Maine, named this isolated monadnock the Greatest Mountain because they believed it represented a spiritual birthplace and, as such, its flanks and summit were sacred. Protecting it was a birdlike creature, known as Pamola, that had wings, clawed feet, and the head of a moose. Pamola was so fierce it could devour anyone foolish enough to attempt a summit.

The menacing mountain god was not enough to prevent others from attempting to climb Katahdin, one of whom was Henry David Thoreau. In 1846, lost in fog, Thoreau failed to reach the top, but he found the surrounding wilds so rugged and unlike Concord that he wrote in *The Maine Woods* (published in 1864), "This was that Earth of which we have heard, made out of Chaos and Old Night. Here was no man's garden, but the unhandselled globe. It was not lawn, nor pasture, nor mead, nor woodland, nor lea, nor arable, nor waste-land."

This raw wilderness is what Maine's governor Percival Baxter set out to preserve when he bought and donated 6,000 acres of land that included Mount Katahdin to the people of Maine in 1931. "Katahdin, in all its glory,

WILDLIFE SIGHTING

Northern Maine is densely populated with moose, an ungulate on the decline across the nation. At Togue Pond Gatehouse, pick up a "Moose Pass," an access pass that's good for three hours, enough time to hike the 1.5-mile out-and-back Sandy Stream Pond Trail, along which moose are frequently sighted.

OPPOSITE: You may find yourself above the clouds on the summit of Mount Katahdin.

PAGES 198–199: The trail will take you past Roaring Brook in Baxter State Park.

forever shall remain the mountain of the people of Maine," he proclaimed. Today Baxter State Park is a sprawling 209,644 acres of lakes and mountains with no electricity, running water, or paved roads. Admission is free to in-state residents. Out-of-state visitors are welcome to climb Katahdin, which requires a scramble along a ridgeline with multiple summits. But they must respect the rules of the wilderness, pay the park entrance fee, and reserve a parking space in advance at one of three trailheads that access Mount Katahdin.

One particularly beautiful and challenging route is a loop stitched together with four major trails that begins and ends at Roaring Brook Campground. Starting with the Chimney Pond Trail, it slowly climbs for 3.3 miles, following boulder-strewn Roaring Brook and passing a few ponds to Chimney Pond Campground, where there's a rewarding (and stunning) view to the rugged cirque that forms the tablelike summit of Katahdin, towering overhead.

From the campground it's a vertical push

CONSERVATION HIGHLIGHT

Visionary governor Percival Baxter slowly pieced together this park, which is now 209,644 acres large, then donated it to the people of Maine. Unlike other state parks, Baxter is completely self-funded by a trust set up by the governor, who passionately believed that preservation of the ecosystem is the priority and recreation is secondary.

ABOVE: Hike along Mount Katahdin's ridgeline on the Knife Edge Trail.

OPPOSITE: Moose are the state animal of Maine, but they're rarely seen—only a lucky few hikers spot them each year. Keep your distance.

straight up the steep and exposed Cathedral Trail, so named for the three rock promontories, marked by blue blazes, which can be scrambled up—but are slippery when wet. Cathedral merges with a ridgeline aptly named the Knife-Edge Trail. Often shrouded in mist and dropping 1,500 feet to the valley below, the tightrope-like trail has portions that require very deliberate foot placement and can feel devilish at times, especially when the wind and weather kick in, which is known to happen with some regularity in north-central Maine. The payoff, however, is a stunning link-up of summits, first to the high point, 5,268-foot Baxter Peak, then to 5,240-foot South Peak, 4,892-foot Chimney Peak, and finally 4,919-foot Pamola—named after the fierce spirit—and the gateway to the long descent on the Helon Taylor Trail, which is oftentimes lined by blueberries in the height of summer, a welcome reward after what can be a harrowing climb.

MASSACHUSETTS

MIDSTATE TRAIL

Classic New England Character

DISTANCE: 92 miles one-way **LENGTH OF TRIP:** 3 to 5 days **BEST TIME TO GO:** Fall
DIFFICULTY: Moderate

Conceived of in the 1920s by local "trampers" who wanted a place to hike, snowshoe, and ski just outside their backyards, the original Midstate Trail was 18 miles, connecting Wachusett Mountain in the north to Mount Watatic, just south of the New Hampshire-Massachusetts border. Over the years the trail stopped being used and was overgrown, until a group of citizens came together in 1972 to form the Midstate Trail Committee with a vision to extend the path to Rhode Island.

Today, the Midstate Trail is an iconic fixture that cuts through the heart of Massachusetts, stretching from border to border for 92 miles. The beauty of the trail is that, while the state is the third most densely populated in the nation, with seven million residents and an average of 839.4 people per square mile, the trail has managed to maintain the character of old rural New England. Hikers will traverse a cow pasture, close the gate behind them, and then maybe not see another soul for miles.

Unlike trails in New Hampshire or Vermont where hikers summit peaks upwards of 6,000 feet, the Midstate Trail has a less precipitous, more undulating profile. The highest point is 2,006-foot Wachusett Mountain, which is still high enough to view the Boston skyline 45 miles to the east. Near the summit is a 160-acre swath of phenomenal old-growth forest of

OPPOSITE: The view from the top of the Midstate Trail sweeps all the way to New Hampshire.

PAGES 204-205: Autumn colors glow below Mount Wachusett in Princeton.

yellow birch, red oak, eastern hemlock, pignut hickory, sugar maple, red maple, and red spruce that glow red, orange, and yellow in autumn. Some trees are estimated to be 400 years old, alive when the land was still inhabited by the Nipmuc and Wampanoag peoples, who gave the mountain its name.

Between high points and historic sites, the trail is a beautiful mix of forest, swamp, lake shorelines, and agricultural land, some of which is surrounded by crumbling stone walls that were built two centuries ago. Two wildlife sanctuaries affiliated with Mass Audubon (formerly the Massachusetts Audubon Society) along the way are habitat for an array of animals from great blue herons to black bears. The trail also traverses parts of Leominster State Forest.

It may be rugged, but the path is well maintained by a crew of volunteers. There are also "a lot of people who go out and pick up or clear trees and then disappear, and we have no idea who did it," says Mike Peckar, chairman of the Midstate Trail Committee. "There are a lot of trail angels out there."

HISTORICAL FOOTNOTE

The trail passes historic sites like Rider Tavern on Stafford Street in the Northside Village Historic District of Charlton. Built around 1797, the old hotel and bar was visited in 1824 by the Marquis de Lafayette, the French major general who fought alongside George Washington in the Revolutionary War.

MASSACHUSETTS

BATTLE ROAD TRAIL

Reliving the Revolution at Minute Man National Historical Park

DISTANCE: 5 miles one-way **LENGTH OF TRIP:** 2 hours **BEST TIME TO GO:** May to October
DIFFICULTY: Easy

By middle school, most kids will have learned about "the shot heard round the world," the moment on April 19, 1775, that so famously marked the beginning of the American Revolution, memorialized by Ralph Waldo Emerson in the first stanza of his "Concord Hymn." The complex and fascinating events that led to this mythologized shot can be explored at Minute Man National Historical Park, especially along Battle Road, a five-mile path that follows a portion of the running battle between the colonists and the British that raged for 16 miles from Concord to Boston.

Today the historic gravel road stretches from Concord to Lexington and winds through a thick deciduous forest filled with turkeys, foxes, and coyotes. Recently resurfaced with clay and sand, it's smooth enough to walk along in street shoes. During the time of the battle, however, this was agricultural land dotted by farmhouses and interspersed with villages, where colonists were rumored to be stockpiling canons and supplies to use against the British. The landscape may have changed, but many structures along Battle Road, like the Nathan Meriam House, built in 1705, have been preserved. The house, which stands at the crossroads where the British column was first attacked by colonists on their return march to Boston in 1775, brings life to the rolling battle that led to a seven-year war.

OPPOSITE: The North Bridge leads to the 1836 Battle Monument in Minute Man National Historical Park.

MASSACHUSETTS AND CONNECTICUT

NEW ENGLAND NATIONAL SCENIC TRAIL

From Forest to Village to River Valley

DISTANCE: 235 miles one-way **LENGTH OF TRIP:** 10 to 20 days **BEST TIME TO GO:** May to October **DIFFICULTY:** Moderate

To complete this beautiful yet unconventional trek that begins at Long Island Sound and blazes north through historic villages, pastoral farmland, thick forests, and river valleys to the Massachusetts–New Hampshire border, hikers need to be on their best behavior. Unlike other national scenic trails, which exist primarily on wide-open public lands, the New England National Scenic Trail passes through 41 communities and exists thanks to the cooperation of a complex puzzle of landowners, from private citizens to municipalities to universities to corporations.

Their cooperation has allowed for the continuous New England National Scenic Trail, established in 2009 and composed mostly of three historic trails: the Metacomet (page 184), Mattabesett, and Monadnock. The result is a fascinating opportunity to travel back in time to precontact and postcolonial America, across the traditional lands of more than a half dozen tribal nations to summit peaks topped by castle complexes, and through the backyard of a historic colonial revival–style mansion where trekkers can view a Monet.

In recent years, tribal consultant and Indigenous archaeologist Jay Levy has established an interactive map of Native history for the Connecticut portion of the trail that highlights key points. These include the precontact village of

OPPOSITE: Stop to tour Connecticut's Castle Craig in Hubbard Park.

PAGES 210–211: Pause at Buff Head Ridge along the Mattabesett Trail for the panorama.

Sachem's Head; the site of a Quinnipiac Indian village led by a female sachem (chief) named Shaumpishuh at the time of contact with Europeans; and cave sites where hunting parties would camp while tracking the elk, moose, mountain lions, and wolves that once inhabited the region.

Adding another layer of history, many sites along the trail, such as the Henry Whitfield House, provide a glimpse into the lives of the first colonists. Built in 1639 and named after a Puritan minister who ultimately returned to England, the oldest stone house in New England was constructed of stones that were quarried from a nearby swamp and mortared with clay and oyster shells.

Between these historical moments, the trail also offers an opportunity to find space and solitude in one of the most densely populated areas of the country. There are sublime western views from steep traprock ridges, two major river crossings, and a traverse of the rugged Seven Sisters range in Massachusetts, where basalt knobs are interspersed with dense oak forests. When the going gets rough, the trail passes multiple towns that beckon with quaint inns where a hot shower and a delicious meal are a credit card swipe away.

KNOW BEFORE YOU GO

Because of the trail's proximity to urban areas and the complexity of land ownership, it currently has limited overnight camping options. There are six overnight sites in Massachusetts and four in Connecticut. Where cabins or camping are not an option, thru-hikers must leave the trail and find local accommodations.

NEW HAMPSHIRE

PEMIGEWASSET LOOP

A Hike as Rewarding as It Is Demanding

DISTANCE: 31.2 miles round-trip **LENGTH OF TRIP:** 1 to 3 days **BEST TIME TO GO:** June to mid-October
DIFFICULTY: Strenuous

This big circle that circumnavigates the heart of the 45,000-acre Pemigewasset Wilderness is often deemed one of the most challenging, most beautiful, and most rewarding hikes in the U.S. But how, people ask, can a hike that maxes out at 5,260 feet be so tough when many western U.S. hikes reach summits higher than 14,000 feet?

"The peaks of the Northeast may seem tame compared to their western counterparts," says Mike Mosley, a trails manager for White Mountain National Forest. "But these mountains make a point of punishing people who underestimate them."

The punishment comes in many forms. First, this loop climbs 9,300 feet over some of the steepest and most technical terrain in New England. And even in the summer hikers may run into hurricane-force winds that regularly pummel these ridgelines. Combine the gusts with sudden bursts of rain, sleet, or even snow, and hikers can get hypothermic very quickly.

The major draw of this hike is what also makes it potentially dangerous: the amount of time spent above the tree line. All that exposure offers sublime, panoramic views of the White Mountains, which seem to undulate forever in every direction.

Most hikers start at the Lincoln Woods trailhead and climb in a clockwise direction up the Osseo Trail to Franconia Ridge, the second highest ridgeline

OPPOSITE: If you plan to tackle the loop in a day, pack headlamps for the late return.

PAGES 214-215: Trek above the tree line on the Franconia Ridge traverse.

in New Hampshire and known as one of the toughest, steepest sections of the Appalachian Trail; it's where hikers summit four peaks higher than 4,000 feet—Flume, Liberty, Lincoln, and Lafayette—and climb 3,480 feet in four miles. That's followed by the less challenging Garfield Ridge Trail and the summit of 4,500-foot Mount Garfield. At around this point, hikers—especially those who attempt the route in one day—can feel the burn. But there is still a major payoff ahead: Bondcliff, a dramatic ridgeline with giant blocks of rock cliffs that look like a Jenga game knocked over by a giant.

The views from Bondcliff are sublime, not only because they are so hard-earned, dramatic, and all-encompassing, but also because they overlook a landscape that seems pristine but was once almost entirely deforested. Between 1880 and 1940, logging companies removed more than one million board feet of timber from the surrounding 66,000-acre watershed. In 1907 a fire raged on for days that furthered the damage. In 1984, the Pemigewasset Wilderness was officially designated and has been a model of resilience, sprouting new hardwood forest, ever since.

CONSERVATION HIGHLIGHT

Pemigewasset Wilderness is one of six wilderness areas within White Mountain National Forest. By definition, a wilderness area is "untouched by humans," but that's not the case here. The first humans inhabited the region 10,000 years ago. In the early 20th century there were 72 miles of train line within the Pemigewasset Wilderness alone.

NEW HAMPSHIRE

PRESIDENTIAL TRAVERSE

A Hike for the Ages

DISTANCE: 18.5 miles one-way **LENGTH OF TRIP:** 3 days **BEST TIME TO GO:** June to mid-October
DIFFICULTY: Strenuous

The highest peak in the Northeast, 6,288-foot Mount Washington is proof that one can never judge a mountain by its elevation. This prominent monolith in the White Mountains falls short of making the list of the top 500 highest peaks in the nation, but it ranks at the very top for having the world's worst weather; wind speeds at the summit have been recorded at 231 miles an hour.

Hurricane-force winds are one reason for caution while trekking the Presidential Traverse, which starts in the north at the Appalachia trailhead in Randolph and summits seven of New England's 48 peaks over 4,000 feet—Madison, Adams, Jefferson, Washington, Monroe, Eisenhower, and Pierce—before ending at the Appalachian Mountain Club's Highland Center at Crawford Notch. If hikers are caught in a storm, wayfinding can be nearly impossible, so tune in to Mount Washington Observatory's "Higher Summits Forecast" before setting out.

Yes, this hike can be dangerous. But for those who come prepared, there's a huge payoff, says Mike Mosley, a trails manager for White Mountain National Forest. "Hikers spend a massive portion of their time on this trail taking in awe-inspiring sights as they traverse some of New England's only alpine terrain."

It's a rare opportunity to hike uninterrupted miles above the tree line, from one summit view to another. The alpine environment may seem barren, but

OPPOSITE: Spend the night at Lake of the Clouds Hut, which sits near the summit of Mount Washington.

PAGES 218–219: Hikers will climb seven 4,000-foot peaks on this traverse.

it is teeming with rare vegetation, so staying on the established trail is imperative. Part of the traverse is on the oldest continually maintained recreational footpath in the United States, Crawford Path, an 8.5-mile trail from Crawford Notch to the summit of Mount Washington that has been in use for more than two centuries. Henry David Thoreau hiked it in 1858, stumbling down from the summit in a thick blanket of fog.

This long history of recreational hiking, as well as the desire to protect what is now White Mountain National Forest from fires and further logging, spurred on New England's first conservation organizations such as the Appalachian Mountain Club, established in 1876, and Randolph Mountain Club, established in the early 1900s. Both still partner with the U.S. Forest Service to maintain the trails around the Presidential Range and beyond.

For hikers lucky enough to secure a reservation, the Appalachian Mountain Club maintains three high-country huts along the Presidential Traverse between June and September. They all serve hearty, hot meals and have comfortable beds, which make storms almost enjoyable.

THE CHALLENGE

Weather atop Mount Washington can be very dangerous. In 2024, the summit averaged 33-mile-an-hour winds, with a high of 147 miles an hour. The summit's temperature averages around 28°F, and hikers can encounter ice and snow into June—in 2024, the summit received a total of 332.8 inches of snow. In the winter, the temperature has been recorded as low as minus 47°F.

NEW JERSEY

MOUNT TAMMANY TO SUNFISH POND

Marveling at the Delaware Water Gap

DISTANCE: 10.8-mile loop **LENGTH OF TRIP:** 4 hours **BEST TIME TO GO:** September and October
DIFFICULTY: Moderate

New Jersey is the most densely populated state in the nation, with 1,263 residents per square mile. That's why the long and skinny 70,000-acre green space known as Delaware Water Gap National Recreation Area, which straddles the border between northern New Jersey and Pennsylvania, is such a necessary oasis for people to stretch their legs. This federal land, along with adjoining 6,660-acre Worthington State Forest, has more than 150 miles of hiking trails that lead to tumbling waterfalls, placid lakes, and steep overlooks with vistas to the namesake gap—a 1,000-foot slice through the Appalachian Mountains through which the Middle Delaware National Scenic River flows.

The most iconic hike in the state, the precipitous scramble to the summit of 1,540-foot Mount Tammany starts in the state forest and ends in the national recreation area. It boasts sweeping views over the meandering river and the arresting break that, millions of years ago, was a continuous mountain range. Today, Tammany's twin peak, 1,461-foot Mount Minsi, is across the river in Pennsylvania. For some, this panorama is inspiration enough to turn around and hike back down. For those who want more miles and solitude, extend the hike to Sunfish Pond, a 41-acre teardrop of a lake left behind long ago by a receded glacier.

To reach the pond, hikers return to the state forest along the Tammany

OPPOSITE: Take in sweeping sunset views from the summit of Mount Tammany.

PAGES 222-223: Stroll the tree-lined trails through the recreation area.

Fire Road, built in 1976 after the Dunnfield Creek fire, when flames leaped 100 feet into the air and burned nearly 2,000 acres. Thick with maple, oak, and white pine, the ridgeline trail offers limited views in the summer, but hikers can imagine what life might have been like for the Lenni-Lenape people who hunted these mountain ridges long before the Dutch prospectors moved in to work the copper deposits in the Kittatinny Ridge.

Eventually the fire road intersects with the Buckwood Trail, which leads hikers to an intersection with the Appalachian Trail and Sunfish Pond, one of New Jersey's "seven natural wonders." Carved during the last ice age, this cool lake is naturally acidic, its water suitable only to yellow perch and pumpkinseed yellowfish. It may be tempting to take a dip, but alas, no swimming is allowed here. Instead, take a lap around the north end of the lake on the Appalachian Trail until it intersects with the Dunnfield Creek Trail and cool off by splashing through a multitude of stream crossings before returning to the original trailhead.

GEOLOGY 101

The Delaware Water Gap is a 1,000-foot-deep, pie-shaped wedge through the Appalachian Mountains that formed over millions of years. It's a half mile wide at river's edge and more than twice as wide at the top, measuring one mile between the Blue Mountains of Pennsylvania and New Jersey's Kittatinny Ridge.

NEW YORK

ALGONQUIN TRAIL

Channeling Bob Marshall in the Adirondacks

DISTANCE: 10.3 miles out and back **LENGTH OF TRIP:** 8 to 10 hours **BEST TIME TO GO:** July to October **DIFFICULTY:** Strenuous

"After a strenuous tussle with windfall and mountain balsam, the trailless summit of Wright was reached just as the sun was dipping behind the distant mountains ... and the entire panorama ... was tinted by a reddish purple glow," wrote Bob Marshall, who would go on to found the Wilderness Society, a nonprofit that has successfully protected nearly 112 acres of public land across 44 states since 1935. Along with his brother and a friend, Marshall was the first to climb the 46 High Peaks of the Adirondacks, a feat he completed in 1925. On July 16, 1932, Marshall ascended 14 peaks—including Iroquois, MacIntyre (now known as Algonquin), and Wright—on a day that was "crystal clear ... as only occurs occasionally in an entire Adirondack summer."

Follow in the legendary forester's footsteps and string together three of the four peaks of the MacIntyre Range. The trail begins with a short, steep climb above the tree line to the 4,580-foot summit of Wright (look for debris from the 1962 crash of a WWII-era B-47E strategic bomber). Next in line is 5,114-foot Algonquin, the second highest peak in New York. The final push is to the summit of 4,840-foot Iroquois. The payoff for a robust 4,000 feet of climbing is 360-degree views of surrounding High Peaks. Plus, as Marshall wrote after his epic 14-peak string, "a thoroughly glorious time out of the entire day."

OPPOSITE: The Adirondack High Peaks burst with color in the fall.

NEW YORK

GREAT RANGE TRAVERSE

A High Peak Challenge

DISTANCE: 25 miles **LENGTH OF TRIP:** 1 to 3 days **BEST TIME TO GO:** August to mid-October
DIFFICULTY: Strenuous

For fit, experienced, and aspiring 46ers—hikers attempting to tag all 46 of the Adirondack High Peaks—this traverse is an awesomely challenging way to knock off 10 summits, eight of which are higher than 4,000 feet, including 5,344-foot Mount Marcy, New York's tallest peak. It's also a way to connect with a rich legacy of peak baggers: the Adirondack 46ers, a nonprofit organization with more than 16,000 registered members who volunteer to maintain the trails and host various workshops. The first iteration of the club was formed in 1937, a dozen years after brothers Bob and George Marshall, along with their guide Herbert Clark, completed their quest to climb every Adirondack peak 4,000 feet and higher. They began with 4,867-foot Whiteface Mountain in 1918 and ended with 4,040-foot Mount Emmons in 1925.

For most hikers, it makes sense to start the Great Range Traverse in the east at the Rooster Comb trailhead in Keene Valley, warming up to the final Mount Marcy summit by climbing a few lower, albeit extremely challenging, peaks. From a bird's-eye view, the traverse dips southwest, forming an enormous V. It reaches its southernmost point at the summit of 4,960-foot Haystack, which offers unfettered views of Mount Marcy. Even before hikers reach the top of Haystack, however, the route poses some of the most intense challenges of the traverse, including a steep, bald descent, assisted by a

OPPOSITE: Take on steep, rocky slopes and beautiful surroundings on Gothics Mountain.

PAGES 228-229: Adirondack Park is the ultimate playground for both day and long-distance hikers.

cable handhold amid what appears to be an old avalanche slide from the summit of 4,736-foot Gothics. On the backside of the next peak over, 4,515-foot Saddleback Mountain, the traverse requires a scrambling descent over steep ledges before climbing again to the summit of 4,827-foot Basin Mountain, where hikers will find a stunning perspective of the precipitous cliffs on Saddleback. In total, the traverse gains 10,000 feet of elevation before the final descent, where it spits hikers out at the Adirondack Mountain Club's Adirondack Loj, a cabin with private and bunk rooms for up to 38 people at Heart Lake.

The traverse is steep, rugged, and technical. But it's also beloved, not only for its glorious, intimate views of so many majestic peaks, but also because it allows hikers a sense of timelessness. This is a chance to immerse yourself in the heart of the High Peaks Wilderness, a rugged landscape and peaceful alternative to the frenetic action of New York City and the dense populations of the eastern seaboard. For an especially vibrant show, attempt the traverse when autumn colors are at their height in late September.

THE CHALLENGE

Nordic skiing Olympic gold medalist Jessie Diggins ran this traverse for her annual "Big Stupid," a one-day epic adventure that pushes her limits. The point of these adventures, she says, is "so that if I ever doubt myself the night before a big race, I can think back on it and know that I am made of tougher stuff."

PENNSYLVANIA

STANDING STONE TRAIL

The Cradle of Industrial Development

DISTANCE: 85 miles one-way **LENGTH OF TRIP:** 4 to 5 days **BEST TIME TO GO:** Fall
DIFFICULTY: Moderate

Roughly halfway between Pittsburgh and Philadelphia, running north to south through Central Pennsylvania, the Standing Stone Trail follows the ridgeline along the northern terminus of the ancient Appalachian Mountains. Its rocky outcrops, 800 feet high, provide sweeping views of undulating hills carpeted with hardwood forests, 350-million-year-old sandstone formations, and small towns surrounded by agricultural lands.

In the south, the trail starts at Cowans Gap State Park, which, like all Pennsylvania state parks, offers free admission. Winding north the trail passes through multiple parcels of public land, including Rocky Ridge Natural Area. With showy orchids and pink and yellow lady's slippers that sprout between Oriskany sandstone and limestone formations , the area attracts both flower lovers and rock climbers.

Surrounded by such a peaceful, pastoral landscape you'll find it almost impossible to comprehend that in the 18th and 19th centuries, central Pennsylvania was stripped of its white pine, hemlock, and hardwoods to create charcoal that fueled blast furnaces for iron. In the 1900s, the region was quarried for silica, sand that was turned into bricks to line the steel furnaces in Bethlehem and Pittsburgh until the 1950s.

"Pennsylvania is the cradle of industrial development within the country," says George H. Conrad III, president of the Standing Stone Trail Club.

OPPOSITE: Mountain laurel, Pennsylvania's state flower, blooms in Cowans Gap State Park.

PAGES 232-233: Hike the Thousand Steps, a narrow sandstone path, through the trees.

"When you're hiking in these woods, you're bound to come across interesting historical things."

If they know where to look, hikers will find remnants of charcoal hearths where fires once smoldered all summer long under a sludge of mud and leaves; railroad spikes discarded from the construction of the South Pennsylvania Railroad, a project that was never completed; and broken cart wheels left behind along centuries-old thoroughfares.

The most prominent industrial remnant is the Thousand Steps, a series of 1,037 sandstone steps that rises 850 feet over a half mile to a site where workers once quarried ganister, a fine-grained sandstone used to produce silica bricks. At the top of this staircase are views to verdant peaks and the meandering Juniata River far below. The steps come roughly near the halfway mark between the towns of Huntingdon and Mount Union and are considered the most difficult part of the hike.

As difficult as it may be to imagine today, "there's hardly any place in the country where there has been so much human involvement in the environment," says Conrad. "Everything that came out of here went to Philadelphia or other urban areas."

HISTORICAL FOOTNOTE

The Thousand Steps were constructed in 1936 by employees of Harbison-Walker Refractories, a Pittsburgh company that manufactured silica bricks. The workers would carry ganister down the stairs from the quarry at the top. The resulting bricks were used to line furnaces that fueled steel production through World War II.

RHODE ISLAND

CLIFF WALK NATIONAL RECREATION TRAIL

A Stroll Through the Gilded Age

DISTANCE: 3.5 miles one-way **LENGTH OF TRIP:** 1 to 3 hours **BEST TIME TO GO:** Year-round **DIFFICULTY:** Easy

Greet the rising sun with the same view over Rhode Island Sound and the Atlantic Ocean that the Vanderbilts would have had from their formidable mansion, the Breakers, one of many Gilded Age "cottages" that line the storied Cliff Walk in Newport. While not exactly a rigorous hike, this shoreline path—starting at Easton's Beach in the north and hugging a curvaceous shoreline on pavement, through tunnels, and across boulders, before ending at Bailey's Beach in the south—offers an intimate view of America's opulent past.

Once a footpath for the Narragansett Indians, and later a place for colonists to scavenge the spoils of shipwrecks, the Cliff Walk now fronts manicured lawns, some the length of a football field, that lead to summer getaways for the wealthiest of New Yorkers. These scions of banking, real estate, manufacturing, and trade, who began building their mansions on this peninsula in the latter half of the 1800s, vacationed here in a real-life Gatsbyesque circuit.

The most famous homes are open to the public as museums, including the Breakers, an Italianate palazzo built in 1895 for Cornelius Vanderbilt II, and Rosecliff, built in 1902 for silver heiress Theresa Fair Oelrichs and modeled after the garden retreat Grand Trianon at Versailles. Others have been put to

OPPOSITE: The public-access walk takes hikers and strollers past Gilded Age mansions.

PAGES 236-237: Ochre Court cost $4.5 million to build when it was constructed in 1892.

different use, such as Ochre Court, a French Gothic estate once home to real estate magnate Ogden Goulet that is now the admissions building for Salve Regina University.

Many homes along this storied walk are still privately owned—so it's a small miracle that the path still exists. Over the past century and a half, some homeowners have built walls, planted trees, or posted guard dogs to keep walkers away. Others have built tunnels to allow smooth passage for hikers while protecting views. The path has been pummeled by hurricanes and slowly eroded by crashing waves.

Despite the challenges, the path remains a beloved public space and open-air museum. In total, there are 16 official markers along the way, each with a QR code that hikers can scan to learn more. Stop 12, for example, is the cliffside Chinese Tea House, modeled after the architecture of the Song dynasty. Today it's a restaurant, but it once served as a gathering place for Alva Erskine Belmont (formerly Vanderbilt) to host women's suffrage rallies.

POST-HIKE ACTIVITY

Check in to the Gilded Age at the Chanler at Cliff Walk, a five-star hotel that was once the home of New York congressman John Winthrop Chanler. The only hotel directly on the walk, this elegant oasis offers manicured gardens, ocean views, and a five- or eight-course blind-tasting menu at Cara restaurant.

VERMONT

LONG TRAIL

Inspiration for the Appalachian Trail

DISTANCE: 272 miles one-way **LENGTH OF TRIP:** 20 to 30 days **BEST TIME TO GO:** Late summer to early fall
DIFFICULTY: Strenuous

In 1909, while sitting in a tent on the flanks of Stratton Mountain, James P. Taylor, a Harvard graduate and onetime instructor of pedagogy at Colgate University, devised a plan to build a trail running the length of Vermont along the spine of the Green Mountains from south to north. He founded what would become the Green Mountain Club, and in 1910 construction of his "footpath in the wilderness" began. Completed in 1930, the Long Trail, the oldest continuous footpath in the U.S., was the inspiration behind the Appalachian Trail.

"I wouldn't say that once it was done, it was the best trail," says Green Mountain Club executive director Michael DeBonis. "It used old fire roads, logging roads, and town roads." But over the past century or so, he adds, the club has focused on improving the trail conditions, the environmental quality of the trail, and the hiking experience to create a trail where "there isn't an ugly mile" along the entire route.

The Long Trail cuts through deep hardwood forests that are home to black bears, winds around tranquil beaver ponds where moose gather, and follows creeks leading to cascading falls. High points include bald summits sprouting with dwarf fauna more commonly found in the Arctic tundra and vistas like the Great Cliff, where peregrine falcons are known to nest.

In 1917, the Green Mountain Club's first-ever *Long Trail Guide* advised that men hike the rugged trail in "ordinary height shoes with hobnails, felt hat, generous-size silk bandanna, inch-wide leather belt with cup attached, wool underwear, wool shirt, and stout wool trousers." Women were told

HISTORICAL FOOTNOTE

Built in 1962, Bromley Tower was a 40-foot-tall observation platform atop 3,260-foot Bromley summit. The original structure was torn down in 2012 for safety reasons, and a decade later a new steel tower replaced it, once again offering sweeping views to Killington, Stratton, Okemo, and Glastenbury Mountains.

OPPOSITE: Get your gear ready for a backpacking trip in Vermont's Green Mountains.

PAGES 240-241: The views from Mount Mansfield, Vermont's tallest peak, stretch across the Green Mountains.

to wear high-laced boots and bloomers. Now the guidebook, currently on its 28th edition, offers more high-tech gear recommendations, but the club's mission remains the same: to connect all people with the outdoors.

Apropos to its mission, the Long Trail (with the exception of four miles) is 100 percent permanently protected and managed to ensure that it will remain a free, open resource for all—no permits, reservations, or permissions are necessary to hike or camp at one of its 70 backcountry sites. As of 2024, all pit toilets along the trail were replaced with more environmentally friendly composting privies that turn human waste into soil free of pathogens, making them much more sanitary for hikers and the surrounding environment. Keeping conservation top of mind, Green Mountain National Forest also instituted guidelines on "trail magic." Trail angels must be present to hand out supplies like water bottles and snacks as unattended food can harm wildlife or go bad.

From the border with Massachusetts to Killington, Vermont, the Long Trail and the Appalachian

BY THE NUMBERS

- **20: Percent of people who use the trail and give back to it through donations or volunteering**
- **500: Mileage of the entire Long Trail system including side trails**
- **9,000+: Members of the Green Mountain Club**
- **25,000+: Acres of Vermont forest the Long Trail Protection Campaign has conserved**

ABOVE: Make camp at the top of Mount Abraham.

OPPOSITE: Hike to Libby's Look to watch an epic sunset over the Green Mountains.

Trail coincide for 100 miles. That portion can be crowded in peak summer hiking months. Farther north, at the height of summer, thousands of hikers using a multitude of trails also converge on 4,393-foot Mount Mansfield (page 244), the highest point in Vermont and an iconic stop on the Long Trail. But there are still many oases of solitude, especially north of Mount Mansfield, where the crowds thin out and the trail becomes especially rugged all the way to the Canadian border.

With a total vertical gain of 66,000 feet, a generous amount of mud in the shoulder seasons (affectionately, or at least aptly, called "mud season"), and increasing occurrence of flooding in summer, the Long Trail remains a significant challenge for hikers. But the hardships are mitigated by a trail club that has lasted for more than a century and remains dedicated to maintaining the grandfather of American thru-hikes for centuries to come.

VERMONT

MOUNT MANSFIELD

Green Mountain Tundra via the Sunset Ridge and Laura Cowles Trails

DISTANCE: 4.5-mile loop **LENGTH OF TRIP:** 4 hours **BEST TIME TO GO:** August to October
DIFFICULTY: Moderate

Many trails lead to Vermont's highest peak, 4,393-foot Mount Mansfield in the heart of the Green Mountains. Hiking it is a rite of passage for Vermonters. When viewed from the east, the peak's profile appears to be that of a long-faced human, the summit of which is the chin. This bald schist knob is one of the only places within the continental United States where Ice Age alpine tundra, normally found 2,000 miles farther north, thrives.

For technicolor views of the surrounding Green Mountains, especially when the foliage is popping red, yellow, and orange in the autumn, start on the Eagles Cut Trail in Underhill State Park. After a short hike on a road built by the Civilian Conservation Corps, take the Sunset Ridge Trail, a winding path that leads to the Long Trail (the oldest long-distance footpath in the United States) and the half-mile scramble to the tundralike top. It's imperative to watch your step along the way so as not to crush the hearty but delicate flora underfoot. In addition, there is no camping at the summit and dogs must be leashed to protect the environment. Standing on the exposed summit, you'll see the whole state spread out below, from Lake Champlain to the west and Stowe Mountain Resort to the east to the Lamoille Valley to the north and the state capital of Montpelier to the southeast.

OPPOSITE: Trek to the summit of Mount Mansfield, which reaches 4,393 feet.

VIRGINIA

OLD RAG MOUNTAIN

Shenandoah National Park's Billion-Year-Old Playground

DISTANCE: 9.2 miles round-trip **LENGTH OF TRIP:** 7 to 8 hours **BEST TIME TO GO:** Spring or fall
DIFFICULTY: Strenuous

Beloved Old Rag rises 3,284 feet above the hazy Blue Ridge Mountains, an undulating carpet of green, abundant with trillium, wild ginger, showy orchids, and mountain laurel thick with fragrant pink blossoms in the spring. Named for its underlying Old Rag granite, this bald knob was once part of a billion-year-old mountain range that stretched from Mexico to Canada and was likely as high as the Rockies.

The hike to the top of Old Rag along the Ridge Trail is so popular (upwards of 1,200 people hike it per day) that it requires an advance reservation and timed entry during peak season, from March through November. It also necessitates a scramble through two especially precipitous sections known as the Squeeze and the Chute. To geologists, these fascinating narrows tell the story of how the mountain formed over millions of years. To hikers, the Squeeze appears to be an enormous crack in the granite that is so narrow, it feels like hiking through a cave. The Chute is a natural staircase in the middle of which hovers a massive overhead boulder wedged between two rock walls. At the summit, an exposed outcrop of Old Rag granite, hikers are rewarded with uninterrupted views to the surrounding peaks, the centerpiece of which is 4,049-foot Hawksbill Mountain, the highest point in Shenandoah National Park.

OPPOSITE: Old Rag stands in the distance behind a meadow blooming with mountain laurels.

VIRGINIA TO PENNSYLVANIA

POTOMAC HERITAGE NATIONAL SCENIC TRAIL

Capital History Along the Banks of an Iconic River

DISTANCE: 825 miles one-way **LENGTH OF TRIP:** 4 to 8 weeks **BEST TIME TO GO:** Year-round **DIFFICULTY:** Easy

A 1974 study described the proposed Potomac Heritage National Scenic Trail, officially designated in 1984, as one that "would follow the course of the Potomac River from source to mouth, linking an astounding array of superlative historic, scenic, natural, and cultural features, and offering an outstanding recreation opportunity for the residents of the Potomac Valley and its annual millions of visitors."

While all 825 miles of the proposed trail haven't been connected or completed yet, hikers can tackle portions, including the 184.5-mile Chesapeake & Ohio Canal Towpath, a crushed-rock thoroughfare that connects Georgetown in Washington, D.C., to Cumberland, Maryland. It will take years, however, for this grand vision to be fully realized. A recurring problem with establishing the trail in an area as populated as the D.C. region is that it must travel through land that is expensive and difficult to acquire.

One rugged, section that will give hikers a sense of what this trail could be is the 10-mile-long footpath that winds along the Virginia bank of the Potomac River between Live Oak Drive and Theodore Roosevelt Island. Part of the Atlantic flyway, this portion of the river is a haven for more than 150 species of birds, including great blue herons and Cooper's hawks.

OPPOSITE: Great Falls cascades between Virginia and Maryland. Hikers can walk a shaded boardwalk path over the falls and between the two states.

WEST VIRGINIA

GRANDVIEW RIM TRAIL

An Ancient River, a New Park

DISTANCE: 3.2 miles out and back **LENGTH OF TRIP:** 2 hours **BEST TIME TO GO:** Spring or fall
DIFFICULTY: Moderate

The New River Gorge has been a coveted destination for kayakers, whitewater rafters, anglers, and hikers for decades—so much so that in 1963 the West Virginia House of Delegates passed a resolution trying to establish it as a "national playground." The proposal was set to go all the way to the White House but stalled out after President John F. Kennedy was assassinated. More than a half century later, the "playground" finally got its due when a 72,000-acre swath of land surrounding 52 miles of the New River Gorge was designated a national park in February 2021.

The park's special magic is the river itself. Estimated to be between 300 million and 360 million years old—one of the oldest rivers on the planet—the New River was carving its path through bedrock as the Appalachian Mountains rose up around it. Because it plunges 760 feet over 66 miles and is filled with long, technical Class V rapids, it's among the most challenging and difficult rivers in the country for whitewater paddlers.

One of the best ways to see seven miles of the river and the sweeping drama of the surrounding gorge—and to avoid the crowds that descend on more iconic park destinations like the New River Gorge Bridge farther north—is to hike the Grandview Rim Trail. The river is a precipitous 1,400 feet below the trail but remains within view the entire hike. The trail

OPPOSITE: Enjoy the beauty of a sunset over the New River Gorge.

PAGES 252-253: The New River stretches 320 miles across North Carolina, Virginia, and West Virginia.

carves its path around lush and densely forested ancient mountains that blare gold, red, and orange in the autumn. In spring, portions of the trail are engulfed by hot pink Catawba rhododendrons, and into summer the trail is dotted by the delicate pink and white blooms of mountain laurels.

More than just a jumping-off point into a serene landscape, the Grandview Rim Trail offers a glimpse into the Appalachia of the past when these mountains were logged for timber, mined for coal, booming with small mill towns, and crisscrossed by narrow-gauge railroads. From the main overlook, hikers can see an active railway and the small town of Quinnimont, where the first coal was shipped out of the gorge in 1873. Far below, in the river itself, two massive concrete piers stand erect. They once held a bridge that connected the villages of Glade and Hamlet. As the trees ran out and the timber boom ended, these towns died. The steel bridge was recycled for use in World War II.

HISTORICAL FOOTNOTE

Almost 50 coal mining towns once lined the New River, including Nuttallburg, the site of the largest mine in the New River Coalfield in the late 1800s. In the 1920s, industrialist Henry Ford leased the entire mine to "vertically integrate" his company, gaining control of all aspects of his automobile production.

PART FOUR

THE SOUTH

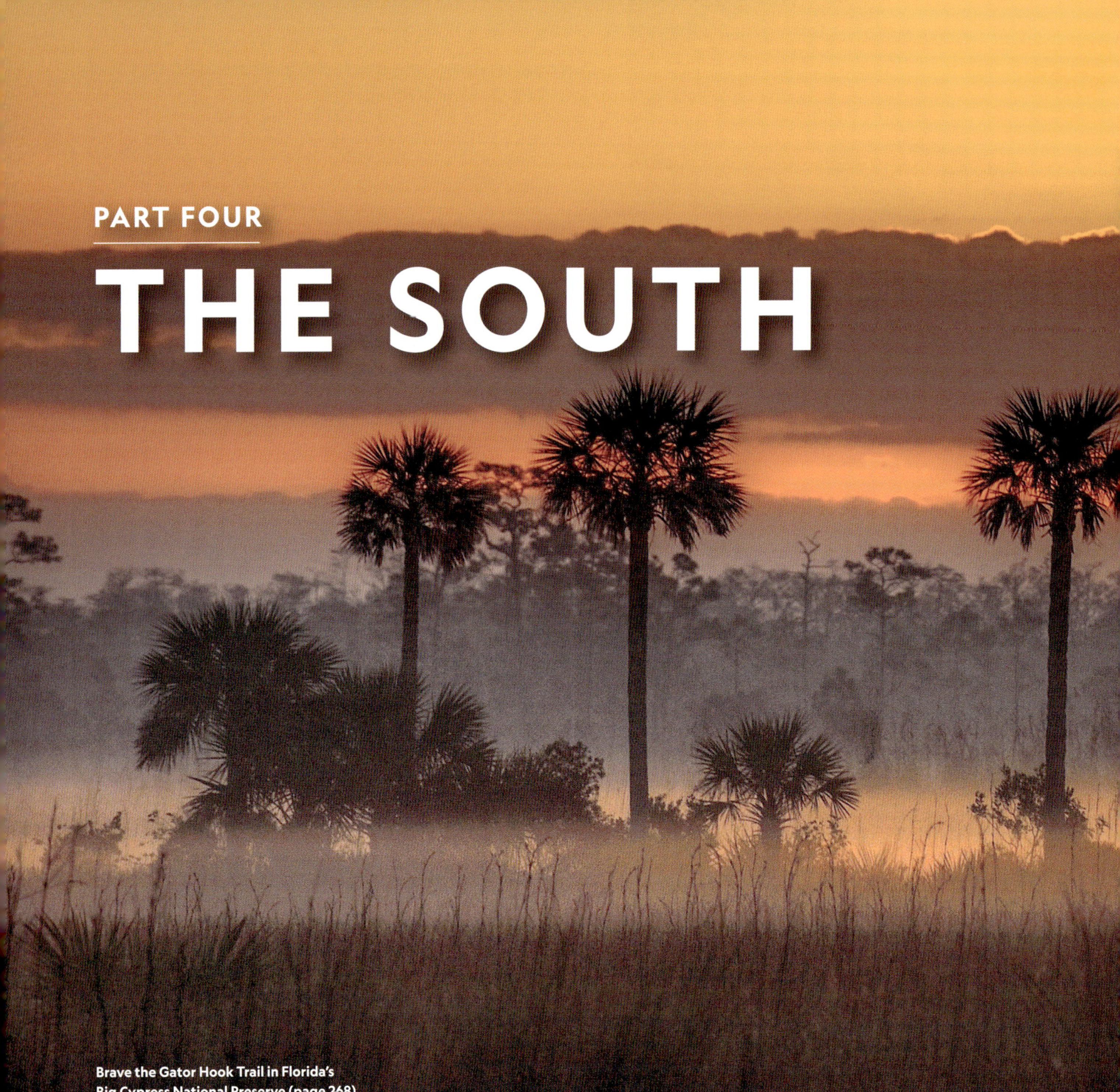

Brave the Gator Hook Trail in Florida's Big Cypress National Preserve (page 268)

ALABAMA

WALLS OF JERICHO TRAIL

An Abundance of Biodiversity

DISTANCE: 7 miles round-trip **LENGTH OF TRIP:** 4 hours **BEST TIME TO GO:** Spring or fall
DIFFICULTY: Moderate

A little-known fact about Alabama for the uninitiated: It's one of the most ecologically diverse states in the country—from the rugged cliffs and tablelands of the Cumberland Plateau in the north all the way to the southeastern plains and white quartz sand beaches of the Gulf of Mexico. One of its least explored ecosystems, until recently, was the 21,453-acre reserve in the northeastern corner of the state that sprawls across the Alabama-Tennessee state line and is known as the Walls of Jericho.

Privately owned until the early aughts, the 12,510-acre Alabama portion of the Walls of Jericho is now owned by the state's Forever Wild Land Trust and managed by the Alabama Department of Conservation and Natural Resources. They began building trails here in 2004 so that hikers and horseback riders could experience the region's treasure trove of biodiversity, from the thick temperate deciduous forest where the state champion yellowwood tree grows to a wide array of fauna, including the multiple species of warblers, salamanders, and bats that make the forest their home. But the prize at the end of this hike is the limestone box canyon for which the reserve is named.

From the Alabama side, the hike into the Walls of Jericho starts at a trailhead near the town of Hytop and descends 1,100 feet from the top of the

OPPOSITE: At the end of the trail, find the Walls of Jericho canyon.

PAGES 258–259: A wooden footbridge offers a dry path across Hurricane Creek for hikers.

Cumberland Plateau, switchbacking northwest toward the Tennessee state line through dense oak, hickory, black walnut, and beech forests. It then crosses Hurricane and Turkey Creeks before reaching an old cemetery where there are still a few legible headstones—presumably belonging to a family who settled nearby in the 19th century. The cemetery is the gateway to the limestone bluff through which Turkey Creek flows. It eventually narrows to an amphitheater, carved out by water erosion over the ages and lined by vertical limestone and quartzite walls. The hike dead-ends at a box canyon with an underground cave system, gurgling springs, and a cascading waterfall, all of which sit across the state line in Tennessee.

The best time of year to do this hike is in late spring when the forest is leafing, the lavender Virginia bluebells are blooming, and the Kentucky warblers are chirping. In the summer the temperature can soar into the triple digits, so it's best to stay away until the temps cool and the forest starts turning color in late September.

CONSERVATION HIGHLIGHT

Near the Walls of Jericho is the Paint Rock River, home to five globally imperiled mussels and 12 globally rare mussels. Two of these species are found nowhere else in the world, and one fish species—the palezone shiner—is confined to only this river and one stream in Kentucky.

ALABAMA

SELMA TO MONTGOMERY NATIONAL HISTORIC TRAIL

In the Footsteps of Giants

DISTANCE: 54 miles one-way **LENGTH OF TRIP:** 3 to 5 days **BEST TIME TO GO:** March **DIFFICULTY:** Moderate

"They told us we wouldn't get here. And there were those who said that we would get here only over their dead bodies, but all the world today knows that we are here and we are standing before the forces of power in the state of Alabama saying, 'We ain't goin' let nobody turn us around.'" Martin Luther King, Jr., spoke these words to a crowd of 25,000 peaceful protesters on March 25, 1965, at the end of a harrowing five-day March from Selma to Montgomery. The 54-mile journey, which followed a day of extreme violence on March 7, known as Bloody Sunday, marked a pivotal point in the civil rights movement. Less than six months later, President Lyndon B. Johnson signed the Voting Rights Act into law.

Most of the trail follows busy U.S. Highway 80, but every March, the Jubilee, a Selma nonprofit, arranges a shortened march. Participants gather at Brown Chapel African Methodist Episcopal Church and march six blocks to the Edmund Pettus Bridge, where police attacked the protesters on Bloody Sunday. In 2015 President Barack Obama joined others to commemorate the 50th anniversary of this brave protest.

OPPOSITE: The historic Edmund Pettus Bridge in Selma was the site of Bloody Sunday, a brutal attack on civil rights marchers.

EDMUND PETTUS BRIDGE

ARKANSAS

EAGLE ROCK LOOP

Meandering Along the Little Missouri River

DISTANCE: 26.8 miles round-trip **LENGTH OF TRIP:** 2 to 3 days **BEST TIME TO GO:** Fall
DIFFICULTY: Moderate

To hike the longest loop trail in Arkansas, located in Ouachita National Forest, is to dance with the Little Missouri River. The trail crosses this national wild and scenic river multiple times along the way, giving hikers a chance to enjoy the small but lovely free-flowing, crystal-clear waterway, which cuts through valleys surrounded by high bluffs with mixed pine hardwood forests and exposed outcroppings of novaculite, an erosion-resistant stone so tough it's used to sharpen steel tools.

The loop comprises three separate trails: the Little Missouri, Athens-Big Fork, and Viles Branch Horse Trails. Most hikers start at the Winding Stairs trailhead on the Little Missouri Trail and hike in a clockwise direction, stopping to enjoy swimming holes and riverside picnic spots along the way and taking advantage of camping opportunities. Take note, however, that what goes down must come back up. The hike traverses nine ridges, most of which are along the Athens–Big Fork section, where the trail runs north to south and the ridges run east to west. In total, hikers will encounter 3,880 challenging feet of elevation gain. Take solace in the fact that 125 years ago one poor U.S. postal worker used this route to deliver mail between the isolated communities of Athens and Big Fork.

OPPOSITE: Forked Mountain stands tall in Ouachita National Forest.

ARKANSAS

OZARK HIGHLANDS TRAIL

A Warm-Up to the Appalachian Trail

DISTANCE: 290 noncontiguous miles (320 proposed) one-way **LENGTH OF TRIP:** 3 to 4 weeks
BEST TIME TO GO: October to May **DIFFICULTY:** Strenuous

Some hikes are so rich they require a lifetime of exploration. In the 1970s, Tim Ernst, a young writer and photographer, started working with the U.S. Forest Service to build a rugged 320-mile trail across northern Arkansas. When the project was abandoned, Ernst received permission to continue building it with an army of volunteers. In 1981 he founded the Ozark Highlands Trail Association and was its president for 28 years. Today he's working on his eighth edition of the *Ozark Highlands Trail Guide* and still maintains a three-mile section of trail that's so pristine no one has ever camped along it.

What is it about this trail that so captured Ernst's imagination? The draw is twofold: First, "it was designed, laid out, and built by hikers," he says. Second, the trail, almost 100 percent of which is forested, is blessedly remote, save for dozens of old settler homesites, most of which consist of a pile of rocks with a chimney sprouting up. In the springtime, however, the surroundings still bloom with daffodils planted by the former occupants.

"So many people who come and do the trail are shocked," says Ernst. "They had no idea we have anything so wild in Arkansas."

When the trail is complete, it will stretch from Lake Fort Smith State Park through the Boston Mountains, run along the Buffalo National River north to Norfork Lake, and end at the Missouri border. (At the Missouri

OPPOSITE: Though rare to see, black bears (and their cubs) make their homes in the Ozark Highlands.

PAGES 266-267: The Ozark Highlands Trail Association meets on Hare Mountain to plan upkeep for the trail.

border the trail will ultimately connect to the yet-to-be completed 430-mile Ozark Trail, page 354.)

Three sections of trail totaling 290 miles are complete. The first continuous section—from Lake Fort Smith State Park through the Boston Mountains and along the Buffalo National River to Dillards Ferry at Arkansas Highway 14—is the longest at 207 miles and offers a wide variety of terrain, from forested ridgetops down to river bottoms with swimming holes and boulders. For thru-hikers who insist on pushing all the way to the Missouri border, there are two large gaps of 13 and 20 miles that require creative bushwhacking, either straight through the forests or by patching together old horse trails and forest service roads. Bring a GPS device—the maple, oak, and hickory trees here are thick and there may not be another soul for miles.

Because it's such an ideal hike to do in the late fall to early spring, many hikers use the trail as a warm-up for a more ambitious thru-hike.

CONSERVATION HIGHLIGHT

Forty-three miles of the trail coexist with the Buffalo River Trail, which follows along the Buffalo National River. The first waterway to be designated a national river (in 1972), the Buffalo flows freely for 135 miles from the Boston Mountains and through the Ozark Mountains until it merges with the White River in Buffalo City. The Buffalo is one of the few undammed rivers remaining in the lower 48.

FLORIDA

GATOR HOOK TRAIL

Wading Through Big Cypress National Preserve

DISTANCE: 5 miles out and back **LENGTH OF TRIP:** 4 hours **BEST TIME TO GO:** December to January
DIFFICULTY: Moderate

"Not many people can say they've walked waist-deep in water where there are alligators lurking about," says Jessica Keller, an interpretive ranger at Big Cypress National Preserve in southern Florida. Many visitors opt out of this hike in the heart of the 729,000-acre Big Cyprus Swamp, a wetland larger than Rhode Island, fearing encounters with snakes, scorpions, or the aforementioned gators. For the brave and curious souls who say yes, however, Keller promises the Gator Hook Trail is an experience of a lifetime, like entering Jurassic Park—minus the dinosaurs.

Anyone with a pair of old tennis shoes, long pants, a sun shirt, a hat, and plenty of water can hike the trail, but first-timers might consider doing a slightly shorter route in the company of an interpretive ranger. Park rangers can allay fears of an alligator attack. (Hint: There's never been one on a human in the preserve.) Just as important, they can also help identify the wild array of flora and fauna that thrive in this vast freshwater ecosystem, which is essential to the health of the Everglades directly to the south.

The Gator Hook Trail meanders over a variety of ecosystems, from wet prairies to the higher, drier elevation of the hardwood hammocks, patches of tropical forest growing with oak, wild cabbage, tamarind, and maple. The environment is also a favorite habitat for panthers and black bears.

OPPOSITE: Aside from the wildlife living in these waters, you'll also find beautiful flora like white water lilies.

PAGES 270-271: It's worth getting a permit for hammock camping in Big Cypress National Preserve to enjoy epic stargazing.

But the real sensory overload begins as hikers descend into the waist-deep (and occasionally deeper) water of the cypress swamp. Unlike the bubbly, murky mud that one might expect, the swamp water is surprisingly clear because the sediment in it takes longer to decompose. Trudging through the swamp's claylike soil, hikers will be surrounded by the purple flowers of pickerelweed and the striking streaks of blue and purple alligator-flag, while the feathery canopy of the cypress forest sways overhead; guppies, Florida gars, and mosquitofish swim within grasp; and roseate spoonbills, great blue herons, and egrets fly above.

The hike may not be as difficult as climbing a mountain, but there are dangers, namely tripping on the spindly root system of a cypress or landing in a gator hole, an underwater depression formed by the elusive reptile, which uses its feet and snout to form the hole to trap prey. It's important to wear shoes that tie. Water shoes can get sucked right off, forever sacrificed to the swamp.

POST-HIKE ACTIVITY

Big Cypress National Preserve contains some of the darkest remaining night skies in the eastern United States. Sign on for a constellation tour, during which rangers guide visitors to the most interesting objects in the heavens, including stars, star clusters, planets, nebulae, and galaxies. Weather-permitting, powerful telescopes are on hand for better viewing.

FLORIDA

FLORIDA NATIONAL SCENIC TRAIL

The Winter Thru-Hike

DISTANCE: 1,500 miles one-way **LENGTH OF TRIP:** 2 months **BEST TIME TO GO:** October to March
DIFFICULTY: Strenuous

What the Florida National Scenic Trail lacks in elevation—its highest point is a whopping 270 feet—it makes up for in a fascinating variety of ecosystems, from the sugar-sand beaches of Gulf Islands National Seashore at the trail's northern terminus in the Florida Panhandle to the infinite expanse and dark skies of Kissimmee Prairie Preserve State Park south of Orlando to the swamps of Big Cypress National Preserve north of Everglades National Park at the trail's southern terminus. For a trail that feels so far removed from humanity for much of the way, it's surprising that most of the state's nearly 23 million residents live within an hour of its tread.

The beauty of this route is that, unlike the Pacific Crest Trail (page 46), Continental Divide Trail (page 80), and Appalachian Trail (page 190), it can be hiked in the winter. And while it may not earn thru-hikers the bragging rights of climbing multiple Mount Everests, it isn't easy either: Much of the trail is on sand or in swamps, or travels through sections hit hard by hurricanes, occasionally requiring a scramble through dense vegetation. This being Florida, there are also alligators, snakes, panthers, black bears, and a beautiful array of birds, from ibises to herons. Hikers might catch a thrilling glimpse of this wildlife, but it's elusive and will generally steer clear, save for the incessantly buzzing mosquitoes.

OPPOSITE: **A great blue heron walks on Fort Pickens Beach in Gulf Islands National Seashore.**

PAGES 274-275: **Along the Florida National Scenic Trail, you'll wade through the waters of Big Cypress Nature Preserve.**

There's no right way to do the Florida National Scenic Trail. Many hikers start at the southern terminus in January and hike northbound, timing their hike to reach the halfway point of White Springs for the annual Florida Trail Fest celebration in early February, where there's live music and plenty of good food. At Ocala National Forest, the trail splits into two and circles east and west around Orlando. Farther south, it splits again around Lake Okeechobee. Both routes are considered fair game for a thru-hike. Because there are almost 400 miles of connective tissue that requires hikers to divert occasionally to pavement, savvy thru-hikers pack a skateboard.

Some of the loveliest sections of the trail are little-known places like Rice Creek, east of Gainesville. In the 1700s, this property was a rice and indigo plantation irrigated by its own set of levees. It's one of the lushest oases along the trail, where wild azaleas bloom, bromeliads hang from tree limbs, and ferns carpet the forest floor. Overhead looms the seventh largest cypress in Florida under a blanket of stars.

THE CHALLENGE

Florida has powerful fauna, including alligators, black bears, and panthers, all of which are elusive and rarely a threat to humans. To ensure it stays that way, pack out all food scraps, avoid filtering water at dusk or dawn, and always give these animals a wide berth if you encounter them.

GEORGIA

CONASAUGA RIVER TRAIL

A Cool Meander

DISTANCE: 13.1 miles one-way **LENGTH OF TRIP:** 1 to 2 days **BEST TIME TO GO:** April to October
DIFFICULTY: Moderate

Meandering through the heart of the mountainous Cohutta Wilderness in northern Georgia, the Conasauga River Trail is *the* place to be during the scorching dog days of summer. The trail crosses the clean, clear river or a tributary 38 times, offering dozens of places to splash, submerge, or stand on the bank and cast for a rainbow trout or redeye bass.

Before the Cohutta became a wilderness in the 1970s, it had a network of railroad tracks owned by the Conasauga River Lumber Company, which logged most of the forest, save for a few old-growth hemlock stands visible along the trail today. That these soaring old evergreens are still alive, even after the 2016 Rough Ridge fire swept through and burned 28,000 acres, is a testament to their resilience.

The trail starts in the south at 3,040-foot Betty Gap, named for a widow who boarded loggers. It quickly descends to the river, where it wanders along an old railroad bed that crisscrosses the waterway for miles. During normal flows, the water is rarely more than knee-high, but after a summer thunderstorm the crossings can be deadly, so steer clear if rain is in the forecast, or it may be a while until you can hike back up the mountain to the northern terminus at Murrays Lake. The trail has a few options for camping, and leashed dogs are welcome.

OPPOSITE: The Conasauga River runs through the Cohutta Wilderness.

GEORGIA

WANDERER MEMORY TRAIL

A Contemplative Hike Through History

DISTANCE: 0.5 mile out and back **LENGTH OF TRIP:** 1 hour **BEST TIME TO GO:** Year-round **DIFFICULTY:** Easy

This half-mile-long, wide and sandy path on the quiet southern end of Jekyll Island, a barrier island off the coast of Georgia, may be short, but it's powerful. The interpretive trail in St. Andrews Beach Park tells the story of a young African boy named Umwalla who was stolen while on an errand to harvest peanuts for his aunt.

Ten-year-old Umwalla was sent to the United States on the *Wanderer,* a luxury vessel retrofitted to smuggle stolen humans after the slave trade had been outlawed. Of the 490 humans smuggled onto the ship, 409 survived the harrowing journey and arrived at Jekyll Island on November 28, 1858. Umwalla was sold to a family who renamed him Lucius Williams.

It's fitting that the *Wanderer* Memory Trail is on St. Andrews Beach. In 1950 it became the first integrated public beach in Georgia after lengthy petitioning by Black residents. Along this contemplative path, hikers can stop at multiple interpretive sites, including a wooden shack no larger than a closet that housed enslaved people; see everyday items such as buckets and washboards they turned into musical instruments; and read more about the fate of Umwalla, who was eventually emancipated.

The trail has eight individual exhibits, and Jekyll Island as a whole was named a Site of Memory by UNESCO's Routes of Enslaved Peoples Project, a multinational effort to discover and share the tragic history of the transatlantic slave trade.

OPPOSITE: Contemplate the history of Jekyll Island while walking the *Wanderer* Memory Trail.

GEORGIA TO NORTH CAROLINA

BENTON MACKAYE TRAIL

A Shorter, Wilder Appalachian Trail

DISTANCE: 288 miles one-way **LENGTH OF TRIP:** 3 weeks **BEST TIME TO GO:** Spring or fall
DIFFICULTY: Moderate to strenuous

In 1921 a forester, Harvard graduate, and lanky New Englander named Benton MacKaye presented a novel idea in a paper titled "An Appalachian Trail: A Project in Regional Planning." In the paper, he stated the need for a long-distance recreational route "to establish a base for more extensive and systematic development of outdoors community life."

A century later his vision for the Appalachian Trail (AT; page 190) has become a model for long-distance paths and a full-blown icon of American independence and freedom. To honor the trail's founder, the Benton MacKaye Trail Association was formed in 1980 with the intention to create a trail that more closely follows the original route he had envisioned for the AT.

The southern terminus of the 288-mile Benton MacKaye Trail (BMT) begins in the same place as the AT—Springer Mountain, Georgia. It then travels north and west through seven wilderness areas, following the western crest of the Blue Ridge Mountains and crossing the AT several times before ending at Big Creek in Great Smoky Mountains National Park.

While it's in the same geographical realm as the AT, the BMT differs greatly in that it is about one-seventh the distance of its elder sibling. It's also much more of a backcountry wilderness trail, with only one shelter along the entire route. The 100 or so annual thru-hikers who attempt the BMT need to carry five to seven days' worth of food because the trail rarely

OPPOSITE: Long Creek Falls cascades just off the Benton MacKaye Trail in the mountains of northern Georgia.

PAGES 282-283: Etta Ettman, former secretary of the Benton MacKaye Trail Association, leads a group of hikers across the Toccoa River.

Greece

crosses a road and has only three designated trail communities for resupply. It's so remote in places that hikers may see only one or two other humans per day.

It's a wonderful adventure to hike the trail in its entirety, but most hikers—families with dogs in tow or collegiate spring breakers on holiday—enjoy it in sections. A few parts of the trail are especially beloved and will be more crowded, such as Owen Vista, near Springer Mountain, which offers lush and sweeping valley views; along the broad and winding Hiwassee River in Tennessee, a great spot for anglers to cast for trout; and in North Carolina before the northern terminus at Fontana Lake in Great Smoky Mountains National Park.

No matter where hikers find themselves along the BMT, one can almost hear the voice of MacKaye, who once said of his grand trail building experiment, "This is not to cut a path and then say—'Ain't it beautiful?' Our job is to open a realm."

POINT OF INTEREST

A symbol of the BMT, the 260-foot-long swinging suspension footbridge over the Toccoa River is an impressive engineering feat and one of the longest foot trail suspension bridges on the East Coast. Built in 1977, it has withstood high and forceful floods, which is increasingly essential in an era of climate change, when many trail bridges have become susceptible to washing out.

KENTUCKY

AUXIER RIDGE TO AUXIER BRANCH TO DOUBLE ARCH TRAILS

Ridge to Ridge in Daniel Boone National Forest

DISTANCE: 7-mile loop **LENGTH OF TRIP:** 3 to 5 hours **BEST TIME TO GO:** September to May **DIFFICULTY:** Moderate

With spectacular red rock formations, towering limestone cliffs, and the largest concentration of natural arches east of the Mississippi River, the Red River Gorge Geologic Area in eastern Kentucky's Daniel Boone National Forest offers a vague resemblance to the red rock landscapes of the West—save for its wooded hollers blooming with wild ginger, dwarf larkspurs, jack-in-the-pulpits, and leafy ferns under a canopy of poplar and beech trees. Hikers and rock climbers flock here to play on this 400-million-year-old rock that has been shaped for eons by wind, water, and other forces.

One of the most challenging hikes in the region connects two parallel ridges with views to Courthouse and Haystack Rocks, two monoliths that tower over the forest and are beloved by trad climbers for their variety of routes. There's also a 1.2-mile spur trail that leads to Double Arch, two sandstone formations stacked on top of each other that naturally frame the fleeting clouds, blue sky, and forest canopy.

OPPOSITE: Kids can explore the big rocks along the family-friendly trail.

PAGES 286-287: Chimney Top Rock peeks out from the trees in the Red River Gorge of Daniel Boone National Forest.

The Auxier Ridge Trail begins with almost instant gratification: After a moderate, rocky climb, the tread follows the top of a limestone ridge where cliffs drop into the forest on either side—so hikers seem to be walking on top of the forest canopy. At the north end of the loop, Courthouse Rock looms before the Auxier Branch Trail winds down into the holler to the refreshingly cool water of Auxier Branch Creek. Then it's a hike up the other side to the Double Arch Trail. A right turn at the top takes hikers a half mile out to the trail's namesake for an exceptional sweeping view of ridgelines that seem to roll on forever. Be sure to stay on the trail; the most frequent search-and-rescue call here is to find hikers who've bushwhacked down a ridgeline to a creek below, assuming they could hike it out to the trailhead, only to discover that the creek ends by cascading down a cliff.

Because this popular hike has a lot of sun exposure along the ridgelines, the best way to enjoy the trail in the summer is to get up and out at sunrise, before the heat, humidity, and deerflies attack. Even better, hike it in autumn when the leaves are changing, in winter when the views are wide open, or in spring when the forest is in bloom.

KNOW BEFORE YOU GO

Deer- and horseflies in the dead heat of midsummer can be nasty here. Female horseflies, especially, are known to cut into flesh with knifelike mouthparts. Be sure to cover up, bring repellent, and time your hike during the hours when the bugs are less active to avoid being eaten alive.

LOUISIANA

BACKBONE TRAIL

Hidden History in Kisatchie National Forest

DISTANCE: 15 miles out and back **LENGTH OF TRIP:** 4 to 6 hours **BEST TIME TO GO:** October to April
DIFFICULTY: Easy to moderate

It's easy to jump to clichés of crawfish, deep-fried beignets, and Mardi Gras celebrations when imagining Louisiana, which is why this midstate hike about 20 miles southwest of Natchitoches (pronounced KNACK-a-tish) in Kisatchie National Forest—the only federally designated forest in the state—is such an interesting anomaly. The hike traverses primarily hardwood loblolly, oak, and magnolia hardwood and longleaf pine forests, punctuated by sandstone bluffs and flat-topped mesas that rise 150 feet—high enough to catch a beautiful sunrise. The hike is so forested that it could almost be mistaken for the Upper Midwest. The history surrounding this region, however, is purely Louisiana.

The town of Natchitoches, named after the Indigenous people whose traditional lands these are, was established in 1714 and is the oldest permanent settlement in the Louisiana Purchase. Soon after, cotton plantations cropped up along the slow-moving Red River. Two of them, Oakland and Magnolia, are now part of Cane River Creole National Historical Park.

In more recent history, Kisatchie National Forest was home to massive U.S. Army training exercises known as the "Louisiana Maneuvers." The September 1941 phase of these years-long field exercises involved 600,000 soldiers divided into two armies who fought across a 30,000-square-mile area in Louisiana and East Texas. At the height of these

OPPOSITE: The Backbone Trail runs through Kisatchie National Forest, which sprawls across 604,000 acres.

PAGES 290–291: Kisatchie National Forest is known for sandstone bluffs and unique landscapes.

maneuvers, portions of Kisatchie National Forest were cleared to build three Army camps, the largest of which, Camp Claiborne, had baseball diamonds, dance clubs, and beauty shops. The war games trained Army officers including Dwight D. Eisenhower and George Patton, who would go on to fight in World War II.

By 1946, the camps were deconstructed, and the land was returned to the national forest, again becoming a sleepy backwoods where residents can recreate. The Backbone Trail is in the 8,700-acre portion of the national forest known as the Kisatchie Hills Wilderness Area, a habitat for armadillos, beavers, rabbits, racoons, and deer. Because the trail is relatively flat and sandy and follows an old roadbed for roughly half the way, it's also a popular trail for runners and horseback riders. A few miles in, hikers will find a typically Louisiana feature, Bayou Cypre, a sand-bottomed stream that must be crossed and can be muddy in the rainy season. Beyond the bayou, the trail starts to climb through the hilliest geography in the state, a few hundred feet to sandstone outcrops, perfect for pitching a tent and watching the sun sink over the horizon.

HISTORICAL FOOTNOTE

Hikers have Caroline Dormon to thank for Kisatchie National Forest. The naturalist, artist, author, and renowned conservationist was known as the "first female forester." In the 1920s, Dormon led the effort to establish this 604,000-acre forest.

MISSISSIPPI

TUXACHANIE NATIONAL HIKING TRAIL

Discovering a Tangible Piece of World War II

DISTANCE: 12 miles one-way **LENGTH OF TRIP:** 4 to 6 hours **BEST TIME TO GO:** Spring or fall **DIFFICULTY:** Easy

History buffs will appreciate that this hike begins on the bed of an old 20th-century narrow-gauge railroad and ends at an abandoned naval rifle range and World War II prisoner-of-war camp that once held German soldiers captured in North Africa. A satellite to one of the four major POW camps in Mississippi that held a total of roughly 20,000 prisoners, the remote camp was for hard labor, where POWs cut timber and cleared land. But they were also served hot, hearty meals and, unlike many of their counterparts, survived the war.

A surprising past might be reason enough to hike this straightforward trail, which begins off U.S. 49 and meanders through De Soto National Forest. But it's also beautiful, passing through plains, savannas, and lowland swamps filled with pitcher plants, palmetto trees, and wild orchids and rising in places to drier ridges of longleaf and slash pine forests. The hike is especially beautiful in March, when azaleas, star anises, violets, and yellow jasmine are in bloom.

At the trail's eastern terminus is a seven-acre lake, the site of the POW camp and naval firing range. All that's left of this military history are eerie concrete ammunition bunkers, but there's still plenty of bass, bluegill, and catfish to catch in the lake.

OPPOSITE: Wake up to a lakefront sunrise in De Soto National Forest.

MISSISSIPPI TO TENNESSEE

NATCHEZ TRACE NATIONAL SCENIC TRAIL

Tracing 10,000 Years of Footsteps

DISTANCE: Full length, 66 noncontiguous miles one-way; Potkopinu section, 3 miles one-way **LENGTH OF TRIP:** Full length, one week; Potkopinu section, 1 to 2 hours **BEST TIME TO GO:** Spring or fall **DIFFICULTY:** Easy

When most people think of "the Trace," they think of the 444-mile-long Natchez Trace Parkway, which connects Natchez, Mississippi, to Nashville, Tennessee. The parkway follows a transportation route that's been in use for 10,000 years, first as a path for Native Americans following bison and other wildlife, and later for groups trading with the Natchez, Chickasaw, and Choctaw Nations, whose traditional homelands these are.

In the late 1700s, the Trace was used by boatmen known as Kaintucks, who floated the Mississippi River south to Natchez to sell goods. Unable to float upriver, they sold their boats and hiked home on the Trace, stopping for the night at "stands," inns that provided safety from outlaws who frequented the path. Throughout the 18th and 19th centuries, the Trace was used to traffic coffles of enslaved people guarded by overseers carrying whips and guns.

Most of the Trace is gone, but there are still sections of the old footpath accessible from the national parkway. One of the most interesting is the southernmost three-mile-long hike known as Potkopinu, or "little valley," because centuries of use by humans and animals have cut a deep trench into the fine-grained soil. In some places the embankments are 20 feet high.

OPPOSITE: A wooden pathway and bridge lead into a cypress tupelo swamp along the Natchez Trace Trail.

NORTH CAROLINA

MOUNTAINS-TO-SEA TRAIL

And Everything in Between

DISTANCE: 1,175 miles one-way **LENGTH OF TRIP:** 3 to 4 months **BEST TIME TO GO:** Spring or fall
DIFFICULTY: Easy to strenuous

In North Carolina, beauty lies around every bend. It's no wonder then that in 1977 the state's secretary of the Department of Natural Resources and Community Development, Howard Lee, envisioned a trail that would not only showcase North Carolina's impressive geography but also unite "people of different backgrounds to share a common purpose—building something which will enhance the lives of our generations and those to come."

A half century and many thousand volunteer hours later, it's possible for hikers to start at the Kuwohi trailhead in Great Smoky Mountains National Park, follow the Blue Ridge Parkway toward the Virginia border, and head into the hilly Piedmont region, through the coastal plains, and all the way to the Outer Banks, where the trail ends on a shifting sand dune at Jockey's Ridge State Park. Roughly 725 miles of this distance is on dirt tread, greenway, U.S. Forest Service roads, or beaches. The rest is stitched together by backroads.

"The cool thing about this trail," says Brent Laurenz, the executive director of the Friends of the Mountains-to-Sea Trail, "is that from its outset it was never designed to be a purely wilderness trail. Part of the goal was to connect the natural beauty of North Carolina, from mountains to swamps to coasts, but also to trace beauty, history, people, cultures, and communities."

The natural highlights are abundant and outstanding, including the popular stretch that follows the existing 13.5-mile Tanawha Trail on

HISTORICAL FOOTNOTE

The trail traverses Roanoke Island, site of the first Union victory of the Civil War in 1861. African Americans who were enslaved on nearby coastal plantations soon sought refuge on the island. One of the Union barracks, known as Hotel d'Afrique, was converted to house more than 40 escaped families.

OPPOSITE: Set up a picnic at Waterrock Knob near the town of Sylvia.

PAGES 298–299: Rough Ridge Lookout near Grandfather Mountain is the spot to be for sunset.

Grandfather Mountain, paralleling the Blue Ridge Parkway on a path that winds through tunnels of mountain laurels and rhododendrons. Along the parkway, however, much of the trail was destroyed by Hurricane Helene in the fall of 2024, when 30 inches of rain combined with 100-mile-an-hour winds, resulted in catastrophic flooding, landslides, and downed trees—the effects of which will be felt for years to come.

Historical highlights along the trail span centuries: Northwest of Raleigh it intersects with a 17th-century footpath, known today as Fish Dam Road, that connected two Native American villages and was used by the Adshusheer, Occaneechi, Sissipahaw, and Saxapahaw to trade their goods. Farther south, where tobacco, cotton, and sweet potatoes grow in abundance, the trail passes through Bentonville Battlefield, where in March 1865 the largest Civil War battle was fought. The trail follows a brick pathway through the center of the railroad town of Roseboro (established 1891), which is lined by a public art installation

KNOW BEFORE YOU GO

Like many thru-hikes, the Mountains-to-Sea Trail is affected by natural disasters, road construction, and other delays that can significantly alter the trail experience. It's wise to use only official guides and interactive maps published by Friends of the Mountains-to-Sea Trail, which monitors these constantly changing dynamics.

ABOVE: The Mountains-to-Sea Trail makes its way through forested paths near Craggy Gardens in Asheville.

OPPOSITE: Explore the dunes at Jockey's Ridge State Park.

featuring paintings commissioned by Raleigh artist Autumn Cobeland.

The Mountains-to-Sea Trail is likely the only thru-hike in the nation where hikers have the option to rest their feet and paddle a river, bypassing sections of the trail in two places. From Smithfield, for example, the Neuse River is narrow and fast, and paddlers will fly past heavily forested shores and the 90-foot-high rock faces in Cliffs of the Neuse State Park and through river towns such as Goldsboro and New Bern. Lower down, the river widens into a 2.5-mile-wide estuary that spits paddlers out—170 miles from where they started—at Pine Cliff Recreation Area, a few miles upriver from Pamlico Sound, to resume the journey on foot. To reach the trail's eastern terminus, however, one more mode of transportation is required: a ferry to the Outer Banks, where hikers can kick off their shoes and walk for miles in white sand.

OKLAHOMA AND ARKANSAS

OUACHITA NATIONAL RECREATION TRAIL

Traversing the Mountains of the Mid-South

DISTANCE: 224 miles one-way **LENGTH OF TRIP:** 10 to 13 days **BEST TIME TO GO:** October to April
DIFFICULTY: Strenuous

There's a quiet, subtle beauty to southeastern Oklahoma and western Arkansas that is oftentimes overlooked by hikers seeking more dramatic sky-touching peaks, pastel-hued canyons, or miles of ocean coastline in states with showier topography. This unsung corner of the mid-South, covered by 1.7-million-acre Ouachita National Forest, contains the highest peaks between the Rockies and the Appalachians with mist-shrouded, low-lying mountains, densely wooded valleys, and sparkling clear streams that are especially striking for the solitude they provide. The best way to experience it is on the Ouachita National Recreation Trail.

"The trail offers fantastic heights, beautiful ravines and valleys, and sections that meander along creeks or rivers," says local resident Bill Stanley, who has led trips along the trail with the organization Ouachita Mountain Hikers. "We'll do a significant climb, up along a hogback ridge, and there are a number of pinnacles that command great views."

Ouachita National Recreation Trail has a state park at each end—Talimena in Oklahoma and Pinnacles in Arkansas—and one near the middle: Arkansas's Queen Wilhelmina, which has a lodge and restaurant for hikers needing a shower and a hot meal. Undulating between 600 and 2,600 feet, and climbing a total elevation of 34,000 feet, the route passes through short-leaf pine and hardwood forests filled with red oak, white oak, hickory, and red gum and by

OPPOSITE: You'll feel like getting lost in the woods along this trail through Ouachita National Forest.

PAGES 304-305: Fog lingers over the valleys of the national forest.

rocky outcrops, or pinnacles, with hazy views of the surrounding low-lying peaks—these are especially magical at sunrise and sunset. An occasional wild turkey, black bear, fox, or coyote may make an appearance, but the animals here are unhabituated to humans and generally steer clear.

Most hikers are taken by the trail's beauty, but it's also beautifully maintained, with easy-to-follow blazes, plentiful signage, and sturdy, well-kept three-sided trail shelters for overnight camping, which were constructed by an army of volunteers from Friends of the Ouachita Trail. Each shelter required about 20 people and 620 volunteer hours to build. They crop up every 10 to 12 miles (except in the two federal wilderness areas the trail traverses). And while hikers may not see another soul for miles, trail angels are in abundance, stocking water caches or providing rides. The Bluebell Café and Country Store in Story, Arkansas, provides a shuttle service throughout the entire trail, free rides to the grocery store to restock, and a full menu of hot meals. There's nothing like a double cheeseburger and fries to replenish calories burned on the trail.

HISTORICAL FOOTNOTE

Art Cowley, a staff recreational specialist for Ouachita National Forest, was known as the "father of the Ouachita Trail," handling planning and construction between 1965 and 1979. He later moved to California, where he planned the 1.3-mile Trail of 100 Giants, which winds through 1,500-year-old trees in Sequoia National Forest.

SOUTH CAROLINA

LAGOON TRAIL

Adrift at Hunting Island State Park

DISTANCE: 2.8 miles out and back **LENGTH OF TRIP:** 1 to 2 hours **BEST TIME TO GO:** January to April
DIFFICULTY: Easy

The belle of South Carolina's state parks, 5,000-acre Hunting Island is an exquisite landscape of maritime forest, salt marshes, and five miles of white sand beaches. Filled with native wildlife—especially of the avian variety—the park is home to egrets, herons, pelicans, woodpeckers, and a litany of sea- and shorebirds, such as the threatened piping plover, which winters here before migrating north in the spring. The northern end of the beach is a designated shorebird sanctuary and off-limits to cars and pets.

The park's trail system isn't extensive, but it opens an ethereal low country world to visitors. Undeveloped barrier islands like these are disappearing because of development and erosion, so the time to see them is now. The flat, compact-dirt Lagoon Trail winds along the edge of the maritime forest and offers a window into the wildlife found in the lagoon and salt marsh. After completing the out-and-back trail, visitors can cross a footbridge at low tide over a lagoon to Little Hunting Island—a sandy oasis split off from its larger sibling by the forces of Hurricane Matthew in 2016—to check out the eerie ghosts of Boneyard Beach. Erosion and salt water killed the trees in this once thriving maritime forest, leaving a massive array of sun-bleached driftwood that provides erosion control, habitat for wildlife, and a backdrop for artful selfies.

OPPOSITE: A boardwalk helps hikers explore the marshes of Hunting Island.

TENNESSEE

UNICOI TURNPIKE TRAIL

A Walk of Remembrance on the Trail of Tears

DISTANCE: 2.5 miles one-way **LENGTH OF TRIP:** 2 to 3 hours **BEST TIME TO GO:** Year-round
DIFFICULTY: Easy

For thousands of years the Cherokee thrived in the southeastern United States, controlling a 130,000-acre swath of the rugged Appalachians. One of their major transportation routes was a footpath that led from their capital of Chota, near what is now Vonore, Tennessee, through a gap in the mountains to what is now North Carolina, and beyond to rivers that led to the Atlantic Ocean. In 1540, when Spanish explorer Hernando de Soto arrived, he used this trail to trade goods—everything from scissors to blankets to bullets in exchange for deerskin—with the Cherokee.

In the middle of the 18th century, the trail became an inroad for British soldiers and colonial militiamen to enter Cherokee territory during the French and Indian War. By 1813, the path had so greatly opened access from remote Tennessee into the Carolinas and Georgia for settlers that the Cherokee and the U.S. government struck a deal to start charging a toll to use the road, and it became known as the Unicoi Turnpike, with inns, taverns, and stores popping up every dozen or so miles. During the Civil War, one of the toll collectors was murdered by a band of guerrillas called bushwhackers who raided the remote mountain towns.

OPPOSITE: Get a better understanding of the history of this pathway at the Trail of Tears Museum and Memorial in Pulaski.

PAGES 310–311: Enjoy the beautiful views of Beech Gap from the 43-mile Cherohala Skyway.

GILES COUNTY
TRAIL OF TEARS MEMORIAL
The Trail of Tears - Land Route
In 1987, to commemorate this tragic chapter in American history, the United States Congress designated the primary land and water routes of the Cherokee removal as the Trail of Tears National Historic Trail.
removal of the Cherokee people and other American Indian Tribes.
You can visit certified sites, segments, and interpretive facilities along the Trail of Tears National Historic Trail by following the Auto Tour Route. Look for the official trail logo along the way. For further information, see: www.nps.gov/trte.
Tennessee Department of Transportation

When gold was discovered in the 1820s at a spot along the trail named Coker Creek, the U.S. government built a fort to try to control the flood of prospectors. Still, the flood came and settlers pushed to remove the Cherokee from their own land. The pressure became so great that in 1830 President Andrew Jackson signed the Indian Removal Act into law. This path, once the lifeline of the Cherokee Nation, became the first leg of the Trail of Tears, a 4,500-mile-long network of roads on which thousands of Cherokee and other Indigenous peoples were forced to travel by foot, horse, or wagon from North Carolina to reservations in what are now Oklahoma and Arkansas.

Today the 150-mile Unicoi Turnpike motor route approximates the old path. But for those who want to feel what it might have been like to walk the trail, a 2.5-mile section of the original footpath runs through Cherokee National Forest from Unicoi Gap to Doc Rogers Fields. Those who hike this trail through the dense Appalachian forest will be honoring the footsteps of others who came before.

HISTORICAL FOOTNOTE

The Trail of Tears is one of 21 national historic trails in the U.S. These long-distance routes are oftentimes impossible to follow in their entirety from start to finish due to fragmented segments, but they are important in that they commemorate historic paths of travel that changed the country's history and character.

TENNESSEE

MOUNT LE CONTE VIA ALUM CAVE TRAIL

Great Smoky Mountain Highs

DISTANCE: 10.5 miles out and back **LENGTH OF TRIP:** 6 hours to 2 days **BEST TIME TO GO:** Spring or fall
DIFFICULTY: Strenuous

A fact that is amplified about Great Smoky Mountains National Park: It gets more visitors per year than any other U.S. national park—averaging roughly 12 million visitors annually. This number may incite claustrophobia for some hikers, but it's important to remember that in 1934, the year the park was chartered by Congress (it was officially declared a park in 1940), about 80 percent of this 816-square-mile Appalachian mountain landscape had been logged. Had the park not been created, more of it would have been decimated.

For the claustrophobes, it's also good to know that there are a lot more species in the Great Smoky Mountains than just *Homo sapiens*. Ten thousand years ago, as the glaciers were retreating at the end of the last ice age, these ancient peaks and valleys became a haven for plants and animals that were displaced from farther north by the changing climate, resulting in a hotbed of biological diversity and a fresh-air laboratory for scientists who have been documenting plants and animals here for more than a century. The park's species count is currently 19,000—higher than at any other national park in the country—including 200 birds, 100 native trees, 1,500 flowering plants, and numerous large mammals such as black bears.

CLIMATE WATCH

New invasive species in the park—namely the green tree frog and nine-banded armadillo—likely hitched a ride on a vehicle and are now thriving. Park managers have yet to determine whether to let these species settle in or to try to eradicate them as they crowd out native species.

OPPOSITE: The Alum Cave Trail makes its way up Mount Le Conte on a series of log steps.

PAGES 314-315: Take in the sunset atop 6,593-foot Mount Le Conte.

PING

This rich diversity is on display while hiking to the summit of 6,593-foot Mount Le Conte, the third highest peak in the park. The 10.5-mile round-trip hike from the Alum Cave trailhead on Newfound Gap Road is the shortest and most popular hike to the summit, so plan to rise early and catch a park shuttle (most run March to October) rather than stress about finding a parking space in the trailhead lot.

There's much to see on the hike to the summit. A gradual climb along Alum Cave Creek through old-growth forest brings hikers to Arch Rock, a natural mass of black slate through which they must pass to continue to 4,700-foot Inspiration Point, where there's a wide-open view to Little Duck Hawk Ridge, a striking vertical rock formation. Farther up the trail is Alum Cave Bluffs, a towering 75-foot-high rock overhang where peregrine falcons are known to soar. Most hikers turn around at the bluffs, but those who forge ahead will navigate Gracie's Pulpit, a precipitous section named after Gracie McNichol, a woman who summited Mount Le Conte 244 times—89 on horseback, 155 on foot, and the last time at 92 years old.

WILDLIFE SIGHTING

One of 19 species of fireflies that live in the park, the synchronous firefly *(Photinus carolinus)* is the only lightning bug in the U.S. that can synchronize its flashing light patterns as part of a mating display to help females differentiate the males of their species from those of so many other firefly species in the park.

ABOVE: An eastern towhee is just one of many feathered creatures birders can spot along the Alum Cave Trail.

OPPOSITE: Enjoy the scenery—or cool your feet—in the rivers and creeks of the Great Smoky Mountains.

Spoiler alert: The true summit of Mount Le Conte is anticlimactic because it has no views. But there's still reason to keep hiking: LeConte Lodge, which sits in an open glade below the summit and is accessible to guests only by foot. Its predecessor was a 1920s-era tent camp built by tourism entrepreneur Jack Huff to house visiting dignitaries. The lodge now has seven cabins and dorm-style rooms that can fit up to 60 guests, but there's still no running water or electricity. Reservations for this mountaintop inn are hard to get, selling out within minutes of becoming available in October for the following summer. While the setting may be rustic, the experience is luxurious: Guests eat hearty meals by lantern light, cozy up under Hudson Bay wool blankets, and wake up to magical views of the sun as it rises above Shaconage, or "place of misty blue smoke," as the Cherokee named these mountains.

TEXAS

SOUTH RIM LOOP TRAIL AND EMORY PEAK

Breathing Room in Big Bend National Park

DISTANCE: 12.6 miles round-trip **LENGTH OF TRIP:** 1 to 2 days **BEST TIME TO GO:** Year-round **DIFFICULTY:** Strenuous

Canyons, rivers, mountains, and Chihuahuan Desert landscape make up this sprawling 1,252-square-mile park that feels like the last frontier in the lower 48—an empty space to breathe in the sweet smell of desert sage after a rainstorm or gaze up at a night sky so dark that it's an endless carpet of stars.

Humans have been looking up at the sky here for millennia. First it was the Early Archaic people who were pounding stone tools and arrowheads here 10,000 years ago. More recently it was the nomadic Chisos and Jumano peoples, who knew how to find more than 200 sources of food in this harsh desert landscape. Later the Comanche used the region as a base from which to make raids into Mexico into the middle 1800s. The Spanish called the region El Despoblado, or "the unpopulated land," which is still the feeling Big Bend National Park elicits from visitors today.

Geologists consider the park an enormous and confounding puzzle with multiple forces forming the landscape over eons. "According to local legend, after the making of heaven and earth was accomplished, the Creator took all the remaining stone and rubble and tossed it into the remote corners of West Texas," wrote Arthur R. Gómez, a National Park Service historian.

POST-HIKE ACTIVITY

Big Bend National Park has the least light pollution of any national park in the lower 48, making it a stellar stargazing destination. Park rangers offer free guided options, including star parties and moonlight walks. Even with the naked eye, guests can see the Milky Way, constellations, and meteor showers.

OPPOSITE: Casa Grande Butte stands behind agave in Big Bend National Park.

PAGES 320-321: Find sweeping views from the top of Emory Peak.

In some places the rock strata appear to be upside down. In others, rocks do not fit with the areas in which they're found. And Big Bend is the only place in the country where three major geologic mountain-building episodes are preserved and on display—from the southern terminus of the Rocky Mountains to the farthest extent of the basin and range to the edge of the Appalachian Mountains. But right in the heart of the park are pastel-hued peaks that were formed by a series of far more recent volcanic eruptions. These mountains, known as the Chisos, offer some of the most spectacular trails within Big Bend.

Unlike much of the rest of the land in this stark park, the Chisos Mountains are forested with Douglas fir, aspen, Arizona cypress, maple, ponderosa pine, and madrone, prime habitat for wildlife such as Mexican black bears and mountain lions. That shade also appeals to hikers, who start before dawn on this clockwise loop at the Chisos Basin trailhead, climbing the Pinnacles Trail to the base of 7,825-foot Emory Peak, the

WILDLIFE SIGHTING

One might associate an arid, desert environment with reptiles like rattlesnakes. A surprising fact: The park has more species of turtles than it does rattlesnakes. Four of six turtle species that visitors might see include the Texas spiny softshell, the desert box turtle, the Big Bend slider, and the yellow mud turtle. While the Texas tortoise and ornate box turtle also reside here, they are less commonly seen.

ABOVE: Javelinas call the desert of Big Bend home. These opportunistic eaters will ingest almost anything.

OPPOSITE: Gaze out below the Window, as seen from the Boot Canyon Trail.

highest point in the park. Hikers who trust that a steep three-mile round-trip detour won't crush them should take the spur trail to the summit. Those who want to conserve energy can keep hiking on the Boot Canyon Trail, the summer nesting home of Colima warblers and painted redstarts. (These are big-deal destination species for birders, who travel here specifically to see them.)

Eventually, Boot Canyon merges with the South Rim, perhaps the most iconic perch in all the park for its steep cliffs and sweeping panorama from Santa Elena Canyon in the west to the mouth of Boquillas Canyon in the east. Straight to the south, layer upon layer of hazy mountains disappear into Mexico.

The hike eventually descends back to the visitors center on the Laguna Meadow Trail, where the views of the surrounding basin, with its volcanic cliffs and outcrops, are almost as dramatic as those from the top.

TEXAS

GUADALUPE PEAK

Steep and Strenuous in Guadalupe Mountains National Park

DISTANCE: 8.4 miles out and back **LENGTH OF TRIP:** 6 to 8 hours **BEST TIME TO GO:** Spring or fall
DIFFICULTY: Strenuous

The "Top of Texas," Guadalupe Mountains National Park contains four of the highest mountains in the Lone Star State, the tallest of which is 8,751-foot Guadalupe Peak, which rises 3,000 feet from trailhead to summit. Those who reach the top share a common sentiment: "This trail is challenging! Lots of climbing, with uneven, rocky terrain," wrote one reviewer on AllTrails. "Very difficult on the way up and down," reported another. "I laughed, I cried, and wondered why I do this to myself," another joked.

For those still intrigued enough to summit, a few tips: The first mile is the steepest, there's very little shade, switchbacks feel endless, and the wind at the top can blow up to 40 miles an hour. But the view from the peak will temporarily ease the suffering. Nearby is the backside of El Capitan, a sheer 1,000-foot cliff that rises straight from the Chihuahuan Desert floor, and lesser peaks fade into the distance. Stay to watch the sky turn a hazy rainbow of pink and orange as the sun dips below the western horizon.

Save energy for the way down: The descent is a challenge because fatigue sets in after the strenuous ascent and the rocky trail is tough to navigate on tired legs. You'll be thankful for hiking poles as you navigate the rocky downhill path.

OPPOSITE: It's 4.2 steep miles to the top of Guadalupe Peak on this epic trail.

PART FIVE

THE MIDWEST & THE PLAINS

Explore the wonders of North Dakota's Theodore Roosevelt National Park on the Maah Daah Hey Trail (page 360).

ILLINOIS

RIVER TO RIVER TRAIL

The Nexus of the North, South, East, and West

DISTANCE: 160 miles one-way **LENGTH OF TRIP:** 14 days **BEST TIME TO GO:** Spring, fall, or winter
DIFFICULTY: Moderate

Connecting the Ohio River in the east to the mighty Mississippi River in the west, this trail carves a snaky line through southern Illinois's Shawnee National Forest, a rugged landscape of rock outcroppings, oak hickory forests, and razorback canyons that, ironically, was never a place of permanent settlement for its namesake nation. The Shawnee used this land mainly as a place of retreat and refuge from attacks by the Iroquois and encroaching European settlers.

Many hikers will find that the only national forest in Illinois is filled with delightful surprises, with its punchy, rolling terrain and formations like Garden of the Gods, a cluster of sandstone rocks carved by wind and water that appear to be stacked like pancakes.

Roughly 100 thru-hikers per year tackle the River to River Trail, many of whom are here as much for the history as for the scenery. The trail passes Civil War sites, settler homesteads, and famous formations such as Battery Rock, the filming location for *How the West Was Won* (1962). Considering this is Samuel Clemens's territory, trail names tend to be Twain themed. Tradition warrants that westbound hikers collect a small vial of Ohio River water to pour into the Mississippi River when the adventure ends.

OPPOSITE: **Find a spot to watch the sunset at Garden of the Gods Wilderness Recreation Area in Shawnee National Forest.**

INDIANA

COWLES BOG TRAIL

Ponds, Wetlands, and Wild Diversity

DISTANCE: 4.7 miles round-trip **LENGTH OF TRIP:** 2 to 4 hours **BEST TIME TO GO:** Fall
DIFFICULTY: Moderate

Indiana Dunes National Park is proof that the forces of nature can still thrive amid urban sprawl and industry. Steel mills and power plants surround this oasis on the southern shoreline of Lake Michigan, but 1,400 native plant species live within its 15,348 acres of dune complexes, oak savannas, swamps, bogs, marshes, prairies, and rivers.

In 1899, Henry Chandler Cowles, the father of plant ecology, published important research based on his work in what is now the park. Hikers can still see the diversity of habitats and species that produced his groundbreaking studies as they walk along this trail through ponds and wetlands and over sand dunes to the shore of Lake Michigan. Especially lovely on an early morning weekday when the beach-going crowds haven't yet arrived, the path is a quiet reminder that wetlands are critical to a healthy environment, providing habitat for fish, waterfowl, and other wildlife; purifying polluted waters; and helping temper the destructive power of floods and storms.

The trail isn't long, but it's tougher than it looks—walking on sand can be a slog. It's a good idea to pack a lunch and savor the beach time along Lake Michigan (swimming is not allowed here) before the return trip, which requires a hike up a 100-foot sand dune. Be sure to stay on the trail: Poison ivy is especially prevalent along the sunniest sections.

OPPOSITE: Lupine blooms on the paths to the lakeshore of Indiana Dunes National Park.

IOWA

HANGING ROCK TRAIL

Observing the Great Bear

DISTANCE: 7 miles out and back **LENGTH OF TRIP:** 2 to 4 hours **BEST TIME TO GO:** May or October
DIFFICULTY: Easy

Effigy Mounds National Monument sits along a wide stretch of the Mississippi River as it flows through the northeast corner of Iowa. This bucolic bluff country, thick with mature eastern woodland, looks like an idyllic slice of the 21st-century Midwest. Below the forest canopy, however, lie fascinating formations that, upon further inspection, take the shape of familiar animals. These are the largest surviving group of prehistoric mounds in the United States.

Built by prehistoric American Indian peoples who inhabited what is now Wisconsin, Minnesota, Illinois, and Iowa roughly 2,500 to 750 years ago, these earthen structures were used in celebrations or to lay loved ones to rest. Effigy Mounds National Monument holds 206 of these structures, 31 of which are in the form of a bird or a bear. The largest, Great Bear Mound, stretches 137 feet from head to tail and 70 feet wide at its shoulders.

One of the best ways to see Great Bear is to hike the Hanging Rock Trail, a path that parallels the Mississippi River from a ridgeline high above, cutting through a forest of red and white oak, sugar maple, shagbark hickory, walnut, and basswood before dead-ending at a large limestone outcropping known as Hanging Rock, 300 feet above the Mississippi. Great Bear is the first effigy mound hikers will encounter, and it's the largest in the park. Up close it appears to be a low-lying topiary, like one might see in an English

OPPOSITE: Boardwalks make exploring Effigy Mounds National Monument easier.

PAGES 334-335: The mounds are sacred ancient Native American burial and ceremonial grounds.

garden. Seen from above via aerial photography or lidar technology, mounds like the Marching Bear Group, a string of 10 bruins that stride one after the other across the landscape, are unfathomably precise. Farther ahead, the trail takes multiple spurs to views of the Mississippi River. One of these trails leads to Fire Point, a mound with a mysterious layer of burned clay, which was presumably brought up from the river.

Every mound holds mystery. Some descendants of the mound builders believe that the bear and the bird are the guardians of the earth and the sky, respectively, and the mounds were a way to connect the people to the land, the spirit world, and their ancestors. Archaeologists theorize that the mounds may have delineated territories for hunting and gathering. The true meaning may never be discovered, but almost a millennium after they were created, these artistic earthen forms still evoke wonder and curiosity in all who encounter them.

CLIMATE WATCH

The mounds have stood for centuries, but the U.S. Army Corps of Engineers recently announced that they are under dire threat because of climate change and the construction of locks and dams on the Mississippi River. Together these forces have altered the river's hydrology, causing erosion to these irreplaceable burial and ceremonial sites.

KANSAS

SCENIC OVERLOOK-PRAIRIE FIRE-DAVIS TRAIL LOOP

The Healing Expanse of Tallgrass Prairie National Preserve

DISTANCE: 7.2-mile loop **LENGTH OF TRIP:** 3 to 4 hours **BEST TIME TO GO:** April to June or September
DIFFICULTY: Easy

Experience the last of the subtle and powerful beauty of Tallgrass Prairie National Preserve. These waves of grass once covered 170 million acres of North America from the Rocky Mountains to east of the Mississippi and from Saskatchewan, Canada, south to Texas. Today less than 4 percent of that prairie remains, and most of it is in the Flint Hills of Kansas between Wichita and Topeka.

This quiet 11,000-acre oasis in the middle of the country is an excellent way for hikers to exit the frenetic traffic on nearby Interstate 35 and quickly leave their modern stressors behind by simply getting out into grass to hear birds singing, insects chirping, and coyotes howling. During the late spring and summer, the preserve blooms with aromatic asters, deep purple dotted blazing stars, bright yellow compass plants, and sunflowers that meander to the horizon across the rolling landscape.

The popular loop trail traverses the sharp flint that's ubiquitous to this region of Kansas—and the reason the prairie was never plowed under—and passes through two bison pastures (give these ancient ungulates at least 100 yards of space). Open 24 hours, the preserve is especially therapeutic at night under the brilliant blaze of the Milky Way.

OPPOSITE: **A one-room schoolhouse (in the distance) was the place of learning for early settlers in this prairie.**

MICHIGAN

GREENSTONE RIDGE TRAIL

Superior Hiking in Isle Royale National Park

DISTANCE: 40 miles one-way **LENGTH OF TRIP:** 4 to 7 days **BEST TIME TO GO:** July to September
DIFFICULTY: Moderate

Hikers must be committed if they want to tackle this trail in one of the most remote and least visited national parks in the lower 48. With more than 400 islands, Isle Royale National Park encompasses a total area of 850 square miles, four-fifths of which is water and 99 percent of which is designated wilderness. The trail traverses Isle Royale, the largest island in the park, which sits in the northeast corner of Lake Superior. The payoff for the extra logistical planning required to reach the island is a next-level wilderness experience. Hikers will travel through an ecosystem that, as hard as they may have tried over the centuries, humans haven't altered much.

The traditional homeland of the Ojibwe people, Isle Royale—or Minong, a word that originated from *meen-oong*, or the "good place"—has been a source of abundance for 4,500 years. Descendants of the Ojibwe paddled a stretch of almost 20 miles in the frigid water of Lake Superior in birchbark canoes from what is now the mainland of Minnesota to hunt caribou, collect gull eggs, fish, pick blueberries, and mine rich deposits of copper here. The Grand Portage Band of Lake Superior Chippewa still use the islands, an extension of their home, to fish, gather berries, and retreat for spiritual quests.

Europeans and their descendants have long used these islands as well—first throughout the fur trade, later through timber, mining, and fishing

POST-HIKE ACTIVITY

Lake Superior is notoriously cold, and the water around Isle Royale contains shallow reefs. Combine these two factors with infamous foul weather, and these islands can be treacherous to marine traffic. Ten ships over a span of 70 years have sunk very near shore, which makes cold-water wreck diving a thrill.

OPPOSITE: West Chickenbone Campground is an ideal spot to rest for views.

PAGES 340-341: A moose finds solitude and refreshment in the early morning water off Isle Royale.

operations. In 1855, the Soo Locks—a system allowing freighters to make their way between Lakes Michigan and Superior—opened this remote corner of the world to massive ships that would navigate the treacherous reefs around the archipelago. Today there are roughly 25 shipwrecks recorded off Isle Royale, some of which are visible to the naked eye from a passing boat. Most of the remains of the islands' human history, which also includes fishing camp settlements, lighthouses, and mining pits, are scattered around the periphery of the islands, leaving the inland largely untouched. The result: a habitat for Isle Royale's population of moose and its predator, the wolf, to roam.

Ferries and floatplanes are the main methods of transportation into Isle Royale, unless hikers want to brave the trip over in a kayak, sailboat, or private power boat. The public options operate from May to September and will drop hikers at either end of the island. Hikers can access the Greenstone Ridge Trail from Minnesota via the western Windigo Visitor Center or from the Michigan mainland via the eastern Rock Harbor Visitor Center.

WILDLIFE SIGHTING

By 2018, Isle Royale's wolf population had almost entirely died out because of disease and inbreeding. In 2018 and 2019, to balance the overpopulation of moose, the National Park Service relocated wolves from the U.S. and Canadian mainland. From a low of two wolves, the population has rebounded to 30 and continues to grow.

ABOVE: The northern lights dance above Lane Cove Campground on Isle Royale.

OPPOSITE: Make camp at Rock Harbor on Isle Royale.

Between these two busy island hubs, hikers will find quality solitude along the Greenstone Ridge Trail, traversing lowland bogs laden with ferns, finding patches of blueberries ripe for picking in midsummer, and hiking short spur trails to camp on the shoreline of inland lakes filled with walleye. It's not uncommon for hikers to face off with a moose in the lowlands, munching through a steady diet of deciduous and conifer trees—give the large, potentially dangerous animal its space. Most of the trail, however, traverses the Greenstone Ridge, so named for the mineral chlorastrolite, whose small, rounded stone pebbles are found along a multitude of rocky beaches ringing Isle Royale. From the summit of 1,394-foot Mount Desor, hikers can see Lake Superior stretching endlessly toward the horizon, a view that can be a comforting or disconcerting reminder of how far removed this path is from the luxuries of home.

MICHIGAN

DUNES TRAIL

Sand and Sun at Sleeping Bear Dunes National Lakeshore

DISTANCE: 3.5 miles out and back **LENGTH OF TRIP:** 4 to 5 hours
BEST TIME TO GO: May to October or January to February **DIFFICULTY:** Strenuous

The Dune Climb is a summertime ritual for Michiganders. From a parking lot at the base of this 350-foot wall of sand, hikers grind out the steep but relatively short climb to the top of the largest freshwater dune system in the world. But this is only a prelude of what's to come. Five lesser dunes on the plateau stretch on for about a mile before the sands gradually slope to the edge of the Lake Michigan shoreline.

Hikers would be wise to either tumble back down to the parking lot after the first steep climb or pack a picnic if they intend to hike all the way to Lake Michigan and back. Take note: From the top of the second dune, there are another five dunes and 1.5 miles to go to reach the lake. In the heat of summer, the surface temperature of the sand can reach almost 150°F, making shoes an absolute must. A bottle of water or two is also mandatory—there's very little shade along this hike, and while it may sound dreamy to take a dip in the enormous freshwater lake halfway through the trip, rip currents can be dangerous here. For those who climb in summer, come prepared with hats, sunscreen, water, and shoes. Better yet, wait until the snow falls and bring a sled. The national lakeshore only permits sledding (as well as snowboarding and skiing) at the Dune Climb when there is adequate snow cover. Still, when conditions are right, it's a memorable adventure. Snowshoeing, however, is permitted on all snow-covered dunes, fields, and forests.

OPPOSITE: While hiking up the dunes can be a challenge, racing down them is a thrill.

MINNESOTA

BORDER ROUTE TRAIL

Blazing a Path Through the Boundary Waters

DISTANCE: 65 miles one-way **LENGTH OF TRIP:** 7 to 9 days **BEST TIME TO GO:** August to October
DIFFICULTY: Strenuous

The Border Route Trail offers the rare opportunity to hike within the Boundary Waters Canoe Area Wilderness without having to portage a canoe. This rugged backcountry-wilderness trail, a part of the eight-state North Country National Scenic Trail (page 366), follows the U.S.-Canadian border through thick boreal forest along a string of long and skinny lakes that were etched out by glaciers 10,000 years ago.

The trail is the antithesis of manicured. It crosses rugged Canadian shield granite, is often rooty, and can be wet, muddy, and mosquito infested. It's also in a constant state of flux thanks to wildfires, denning beavers, blow-downs, and tornadoes. This may sound like no fun, but volunteers from across the country jump at the opportunity to come here because it requires paddling into a lakeside campsite and working remotely with hand tools for days in one of the most pristine wildernesses remaining in the U.S.

Navigation can be a challenge, and cell phone service is patchy at best, so come prepared with a map and compass and the ability and willingness to bushwhack. The reward is beautiful solitude, patches of blueberries known only to the resident black bears, an occasional moose sighting, and the calming presence of pristine and abundant freshwater lakes.

OPPOSITE: **A rainbow arches over Ottertrack Lake in the Boundary Waters Canoe Area Wilderness.**

MINNESOTA

SUPERIOR HIKING TRAIL

Getting Above the World's Greatest Lake

DISTANCE: 300 miles one-way **LENGTH OF TRIP:** 2 to 4 weeks **BEST TIME TO GO:** June to October
DIFFICULTY: Strenuous

It's a challenge to fathom the enormity of Lake Superior until you gaze at it from a mountaintop along the Superior Hiking Trail. The Big Lake, as locals call it, is the world's largest body of fresh water by surface area. The volume of the four lesser Great Lakes plus three more Lake Eries combined, Lake Superior is a frigid inland sea, with 2,726 miles of shoreline that stretch across three states and one Canadian province. It's so massive and unforgiving that 6,000 wrecked ships are estimated to be submerged within.

The longest path that parallels its shoreline (by far) is the Superior Hiking Trail. It starts at the Minnesota-Wisconsin border south of Duluth and follows a ridgeline north across the ancient volcanic geologic formations known as the North Shore Highlands and Sawtooth Mountains. These ancient peaks—the highest of which is 1,689-foot Moose Mountain near Lutsen—were scoured by glaciers 10,000 years ago, leaving 1.1-billion-year-old bedrock exposed in places and adding rugged, cliffy drama to the thick boreal forest, placid inland lakes, and bogs ringed by hemlocks and fairy tale–like amanita mushrooms. At least two dozen short and stunning rivers steeply descend into Lake Superior along this shoreline, cascading through narrow rock canyons in volumes so abundant that the ensuing cacophony often makes hikers stop in their tracks, mesmerized. The trail runs perpendicular to these rivers and crosses them all, sometimes via a bridge hanging dramatically above a

KNOW BEFORE YOU GO

As Minnesotans love to joke, their state bird is the mosquito, and the runner-up may be the black fly. Especially in the spring and early summer, bring full-length pants and shirts, repellent, and a head net, and avoid wearing the color black, because mosquitoes love it. Better yet, plan a trip for autumn.

OPPOSITE: Take in massive Lake Superior from the cliffs at Palisade Head in Beaver Bay.

PAGES 350–351: Cool off in the Gooseberry River below tumbling cascades.

waterfall. The descents into river valleys and ascents to the ridgeline result in a total of more than 41,000 feet of elevation change, one of the reasons the rocky, rooty path is a particular beast to runners.

Bookended by the lands of two sovereign Ojibwe nations, Fond du Lac (Nagaajiwanaang) to the south and Grand Portage (Gichi Onigaming) to the north, the trail traverses the 1854 Ceded Territory of the Lake Superior Chippewa, a landscape through which its original inhabitants traveled and hunted by canoe using a network of rivers, lakes, and portages. The modern-day trail passes through eight state parks that interpret this Indigenous history, the fur trade that was established in the 1600s, and, later, the largely Scandinavian European immigrants who settled here.

While the trail feels remote—hiking the sections south of Canada near the Boundary Waters Canoe Area Wilderness are as rugged as it gets in the lower 48—it's also urban. Forty-three miles of

BY THE NUMBERS

The trail is used by a variety of recreationists, made up of:

- **0.6% thru-hikers**
- **1.4% rock climbers**
- **4.3% trail runners**
- **14.5% overnight backpackers**
- **22.8% first-time users**
- **43.9% multiple-visits-per-year users**
- **76.3% day hikers**

its southernmost section span Duluth, a city of 87,680 people. Most residents live within five minutes of the trail and many use it to run or hike every day. For a few brief miles the trail converges with Duluth's Lakewalk, a paved path that passes through Canal Park, a thriving center of restaurants, shops, and hotels lining rocky beaches and the iconic Aerial Lift Bridge, a steel behemoth originally built in 1905 and revamped in 1929 that mechanically lifts when ships from around the world enter the Duluth Harbor.

Because Minnesota State Highway 61 parallels the trail (from a good distance), access to trailheads is easy. Six private shuttle companies offer service along the hiking corridor. All are reliable and accessible, one of the many reasons the Superior Hiking Trail is a wise choice for hikers who want to test themselves but still have an out—especially if the mosquitoes are biting.

ABOVE: **Oberg Mountain roars with color in the fall.**

OPPOSITE: **An American red squirrel enjoys a pine cone near Woods Creek.**

MISSOURI

OZARK TRAIL

Meandering Through Mark Twain National Forest

DISTANCE: 430 total noncontiguous miles; 240 contiguous one-way **LENGTH OF TRIP:** 1 to 2 weeks for the 240-mile thru-hike **BEST TIME TO GO:** Year-round **DIFFICULTY:** Moderate

Glance at a map of the 430-mile Ozark Trail, and it might be tough to envision a thru-hike of the entire thing. Though it was established in the 1970s, large sections of the trail are still so disconnected that they may never be part of a contiguous thru-hike. The good news is that the 240 miles of connected trail are so rugged, spectacular, and untraveled that even many St. Louis residents don't know the trail exists.

The northern terminus of the trail's "backbone," segmented into eight sections, begins 85 miles southwest of St. Louis at the Onondaga trailhead and travels south and slightly west through upland oak hardwood forests, permanent springs, caves, ancient volcanic mountains, and national protected streams to the Eleven Point trailhead. Considering that no sign or kiosk marks this southern terminus of the trail, most people start in the north.

Thru-hikers who attempt this backcountry trail—consistently ranked as one of the top 10 in the country—need to come prepared. It's the antithesis of the Appalachian Trail (page 190), where hikers can find refuge in a shelter or pop into the next town along the route to buy a burrito. The 240-mile backbone trail travels through no towns or cities, offers no shelters, and has only three places along the trail where resupply is feasible—meaning that hikers must exit the trail and hike at least a few extra miles out of the way for gear, food, or water refills. The rewards, however, are plentiful: beautiful solitude, days in which hikers may not see another person, distant hills on

OPPOSITE: Lupine and blazing star flowers bloom in Taum Sauk Mountain State Park.

PAGES 356-357: Stop along the trail to marvel at beautiful Rocky Falls.

top of which wild horses roam, and miles of hiking along beautiful, clear rivers.

This being Missouri, where float trips are a favorite year-round pastime, hikers can get creative in how they use the trail to combine it with a river trip. For those who might not have their own boat or pack raft, start at the Onondaga trailhead and hike 12.5 miles on the Courtois trail section to Bass River Resort, a vacation oasis with a lodge and campground. Eat a pizza at the restaurant, take advantage of the opportunity to take a warm shower and spend the night in a bed, then rent a raft, canoe, or kayak and float back down the river to the trailhead. More hardcore hikers can carry a pack raft on their backs and get creative about where they put in and take out along the multiple rivers that the trail crosses.

The nonprofit Ozark Trail Association works with volunteers and organizations including Mark Twain National Forest and the U.S. Army Corps of Engineers to maintain, build, and expand the trail. Individual landowners maintain some sections of the trail.

CONSERVATION HIGHLIGHT

The Ozark Trail crosses the largest fen complex in non-glaciated North America. What is a fen, one might ask? It's a rare, peat-forming wetland created by mineral-rich groundwater that creates springs and "ooze" areas. A fen takes thousands of years to develop and cannot be easily restored once destroyed.

NEBRASKA

SADDLE ROCK TRAIL

A Gateway to the West at Scott's Bluff National Monument

DISTANCE: 3.2 miles out and back **LENGTH OF TRIP:** 1 to 3 hours **BEST TIME TO GO:** Spring or fall
DIFFICULTY: Moderate

On the Western edge of Nebraska where the Great Plains meet the Rocky Mountains, a craggy escarpment juts 800 feet above the North Platte River. For centuries the escarpment has served as a welcoming break to the monotony of the surrounding prairie. Cheyenne and Arapahoe residents called the rock Me-a-pa-te, or "the hill that is hard to go around," and it was used as a point of navigation, renowned for its sheer size. Its modern name, Scott's Bluff, honors Hiram Scott, a fur trapper who in 1828 was left to starve by his expedition party. His remains were mysteriously found a year later at the base of this behemoth rock, which sits 60 miles from where Scott was left to die.

That's a lot to contemplate while climbing 435 vertical feet to the summit of 4,659-foot Scott's Bluff. The first third of the trail crosses the prairie, where you might find western box turtles and rattlesnakes lazing in the sun. The second third of the trail climbs to a hand-carved foot tunnel through the bluff, where cliff swallows plaster mud nests into the walls. The final summit pushes past eroding sandstone and an active rock fall area, so stay on the trail. At the summit, hikers are rewarded with lonesome views to the rugged prairie and North Platte River that have changed little over centuries.

OPPOSITE: Saddle Rock stands out on the trail.

NORTH DAKOTA

MAAH DAAH HEY TRAIL

Beauty in the Badlands

DISTANCE: 144 miles one-way **LENGTH OF TRIP:** 1 to 2 weeks **BEST TIME TO GO:** Spring or fall
DIFFICULTY: Strenuous

"You hear it so many times from people who come from out of state," says Nick Ybarra, founder of the nonprofit Save the Maah Daah Hey. "They ask, 'How good can a trail in North Dakota be?'"

The answer is beyond good. The trail is magical, difficult, and otherworldly. In other words: awesome. There's nothing else in the United States like this rugged, remote backcountry trail that connects the North and South Units of Theodore Roosevelt National Park, then continues south for almost 50 more miles, winding through Badlands terrain that pops out of the surrounding plains like a pastel mirage. As Theodore Roosevelt wrote of the Badlands, "It is here that the romance of my life began."

The intrigue, Ybarra says, derives from "a complicated equation of unexpected beauty, spectacular landscape, and desert-prairie terrain mix." But also, the Maah Daah Hey Trail is dangerously remote, exposed, lacking in fresh water, and perhaps impossible to navigate after a hard rain. For all these reasons, it's both healing to the soul and a place to test your resolve.

Officially opened as a recreation trail in the 1990s and expanded in later years, the Maah Daah Hey has been used for centuries—with portions serving as a trail for wild game, for the Mandan people to travel to war parties, and for National Park Service employees to run a bison back

KNOW BEFORE YOU GO

The geology of this region is a mix of dirt, clay, and sandstone that can turn into concrete-like mud when wet. There are also small rivers and streams to ford and exposed high points over the course of the trail, so watch for thunderstorms or extended rain events before heading out.

OPPOSITE: Sleep under a sky full of stars at Burning Coal Vein on the Maah Daah Hey Trail.

PAGES 362-363: Named after the "conservation president," Theodore Roosevelt National Park offers a lesson in history and geology.

to the park after it had escaped. Named by Gerard Baker, an assistant director of the National Park Service who is also Mandan Hidatsa, Maah Daah Hey means "grandfather."

"'Grandfather' is one whom you learn from," wrote Baker. "This name not only honors the Mandan Tribe, but honors this Trail and what it represents, a get-away, a place to pray, a place to watch the activity of the Badlands, a place to feel the afternoon heat and the morning cool, but most of all it is a place where you can go and be with MAAH-DAAH-HEY."

The trail is magnificent and diverse. In one southern section near Magpie Campground is a half-mile spur trail to the Ice Caves, a sandstone cliff face below which are caverns spackled with ice even in June—the leftover remains of North Dakota's harsh winters. In a section that runs through the national park, herds of bison roam. Farther north are high, flat plateaus of waving grass interspersed with valleys through which the Little Missouri River flows.

Because it's built mainly on soil rather than

CULTURAL HIGHLIGHT

The new Theodore Roosevelt Presidential Library pays homage to the 26th president's environmental vision and "relentless, resilient spirit." Perched dramatically on a mesa near Medora, it aims to be a "people's presidential library" with no books or archives but many immersive exhibits that put visitors "in the arena," as Roosevelt so famously said.

ABOVE: **Take in Painted Canyon from an overlook in the park's South Unit.**

OPPOSITE: **Wild horses still roam throughout Theodore Roosevelt National Park.**

bedrock, the Maah Daah Hey is very difficult to maintain: The grass gets overgrown, and the soil on the tread gets eroded away after a rain or baked in the sun until it cracks and turns to dust. The trail was almost lost to the earth until 2013, when Ybarra and a small group of volunteers began pushing 400-pound, self-propelled brush mowers along its entirety. They've done this work biannually ever since, and the result is a beautiful strip of mowed singletrack running through the Badlands for both hikers and mountain bikers to enjoy.

Another group, the Maah Daah Hey Trail Association, has added water boxes for hikers to stash their own supplies in advance and signposts inscribed with a turtle, the trail's symbol, at the top. Some offer sayings like this one south of Medora: "In every walk with nature one receives far more than he seeks."

NORTH DAKOTA TO VERMONT

NORTH COUNTRY NATIONAL SCENIC TRAIL

Woods, Water, Prairies, and Peaceful Reverie

DISTANCE: 4,800 miles one-way **LENGTH OF TRIP:** 7 to 9 months **BEST TIME TO GO:** Spring or fall
DIFFICULTY: Strenuous

The North Country National Scenic Trail is unique among long-distance hikes in that it does not follow a specific geographic feature like a mountain range. With a western terminus in North Dakota's Lake Sakakawea State Park and an eastern terminus in Vermont's Green Mountains, this northern path is more than double the length of its more famous sibling national scenic trails, the Appalachian Trail (page 190) and Pacific Crest Trail (page 46). Traveling through eight states, the North Country National Scenic Trail allows hikers to see a diverse array of landscapes, ecosystems, and U.S. history unfold, from eastern Adirondack peaks to the Great Lakes to boreal forest to prairie.

The North Country follows historic towpaths and rail trails, paved and dirt roads, and singletrack through state and county parks, national forests, and federal wildernesses. In North Dakota, hikers might find a rare and fragile western prairie fringed orchid in Sheyenne National Grassland or see the sun setting on an undulating western horizon. In Minnesota, they may spot a moose or a black bear or hear the call of a loon while traversing the rugged, rocky trails of the Boundary Waters Canoe Area Wilderness. At Michigan's Pictured Rocks National Lakeshore, they'll walk along the edge of a sandstone

OPPOSITE: Castle Rock overlooks Lake Superior in Michigan's Pictured Rocks National Lakeshore.

PAGES 368-369: Ice blocks form close to the shore of Lake Superior in winter months.

cliff with a bird's-eye view of Lake Michigan 200 feet below. In New York, they can cross the central Adirondacks, passing Lake Champlain.

The subtle moments of discovery along this trail are endless and may include seeing the only waterfall in the state of North Dakota, at the McClusky Canal. Or passing the 45th parallel—the halfway point between the Equator and the North Pole—in northern Michigan. Or traveling through remote and largely unsung Allegheny National Forest in Pennsylvania without seeing another soul. Throughout the trek, hikers will pass remnants of another era, reversing the footsteps of settlers who, after the Civil War, headed west to make their fortunes on the frontier and old timber and mining operations that helped build the nation. While it generally avoids major metro areas like Chicago, the trail does pass through multiple small towns that give hikers a sense of rural America.

The beauty for hikers traveling west to east is that, when they reach the trail's terminus in Vermont and still want more, it intersects with two other iconic paths: Vermont's Long Trail (page 238) and the Appalachian Trail (page 190).

CONSERVATION HIGHLIGHT

An important pillar of the North Country Trail Association's mission is to create a permanent route for nearly 1,500 miles of trail that are not yet secured. A secondary goal is to conserve buffer land around the trail, especially as portions are rerouted or rebuilt after being hit harder and more frequently by fires and hurricanes.

OHIO

BUCKEYE TRAIL

The Great Circle Tour

DISTANCE: 1,454-mile loop **LENGTH OF TRIP:** 3 to 4 months **BEST TIME TO GO:** Year-round
DIFFICULTY: Moderate

In 1958 the writer Merrill Gilfillan proclaimed in *Columbus Dispatch Magazine* that Ohio needed "a public facility where Ohio youth may have an opportunity to find inspiring recreation."

By September 1959, the newly established Buckeye Trail Association had completed the first 20 miles of a trail. One of the first people to hike it was board member Emma "Grandma" Gatewood, the first woman to solo thru-hike the Appalachian Trail, which she did in 1955 at age 67. The all-volunteer association still maintains and promotes the trail.

Today the Buckeye Trail is an enormous 1,454-mile (and growing) loop that traverses a splendid array of Ohio's natural beauty and history. The trail extends from the Fairport Harbor West Breakwater Lighthouse on Lake Erie, which was built in 1871, to the historic canals of Cuyahoga Valley National Park in the north to the Black Hand sandstone cliffs of Hocking Hills State Park and the mysterious Serpent Mound, an effigy mound built roughly 900 years ago by the Fort Ancient culture, in the south. The trail also follows river corridors through Dayton and Akron, revitalizing these cities' urban green spaces and many other towns.

"People take for granted what's in their backyard," says Andrew Bashaw, executive director of the Buckeye Trail Association. "The trail was built by a small group of people who appreciated where they are from."

OPPOSITE: A winter trek along the Bedford Reservation stretch of the trail offers snow globe-like scenery.

SOUTH DAKOTA

CENTENNIAL TRAIL

Through the Soul of the Black Hills

DISTANCE: 125 miles one-way **LENGTH OF TRIP:** 7 to 10 days **BEST TIME TO GO:** Spring or fall
DIFFICULTY: Moderate

It's not uncommon for hikers to get temporarily sidelined by a meandering bison or a scolding prairie dog while hiking through the tallgrass at Wind Cave National Park, at the southern terminus of the Centennial Trail. Farther north, hikers might encounter a bighorn sheep or mountain goat. That's the beauty of this hike—it's in the heart of the Black Hills. Instead of getting caught behind a conga line of vehicle-bound tourists rubbernecking at the stunning scenery along the Needles Highway, as some two million visitors do every year, hikers on the Centennial Trail are sent through the soul of these mountains, which are sacred to their traditional landowners, the Lakota Sioux.

Unveiled in 1989, the 100-year anniversary of South Dakota's statehood, the 89 Trail, as it is also known, starts at Bear Butte State Park in the north and traverses state and federal lands, including Fort Meade Recreation Area, Black Hills National Forest, the Black Elk Wilderness, and Custer State Park, before ending at Wind Cave National Park—passing millions of years of complex geologic history and 10,000 years of known human habitation. The solitude along some points of this trail is so complete that a hiker's only companion is the wind whistling through the ponderosa pines.

The trail's northern terminus, at Bear Butte State Park, sets the contemplative tone for a hike that traverses so much sacred ground. Its namesake

GEOLOGY 101

The Black Hills were formed by the uplifting of Earth's crust millions of years ago. Precambrian rock formations consisting of slate, schist, and granite form its central core. Iconic features like the tallest mountain (7,242-foot Black Elk Peak, page 378) and the nearby Needles and Granite Spires formations are part of this core.

OPPOSITE: American history: To see Mount Rushmore hikers have to take a spur trail.

PAGES 374–375: The sun sets over Sylvan Lake at Custer State Park in the Black Hills.

butte, known as Mato Paha to the Lakota and as Noahvose to the Cheyenne, is a 4,442-foot intrusion of igneous rock called a laccolith, which rises out of the surrounding plains. Many Native Americans believe it is the place where the creator has chosen to communicate with them through visions and prayer, so they pilgrimage to this site to hold religious ceremonies and offer prayer cloths and tobacco ties to their deity. It's important that hikers respect these rituals and do not interfere.

The Black Hills forever changed for the Lakota in 1874, when Lt. Col. George Armstrong Custer's troops found gold. The discovery led to a gold rush and an influx of settlers, violating the 1868 Treaty of Fort Laramie, which had granted the Sioux Nation ownership of the Black Hills. In 1875 the U.S. government offered to buy back the Black Hills for $6 million (approximately $195 million today), but Sioux leader Sitting Bull rejected the offer. The clash ultimately led to the Great Sioux War between the U.S. and Sioux and Cheyenne Tribes culminating in the

CONSERVATION HIGHLIGHT

South Dakota doesn't immediately spring to mind when considering the ancient trees of North America. But deep in the Black Hills grows Rosa, a nearly 800-year-old ponderosa pine. Researchers from the U.S. Forest Service and South Dakota Mines are keeping its location secret so that it can thrive in solitude.

ABOVE: Sunflowers stand tall at sunrise in front of Bear Butte.

OPPOSITE: American bison graze in the tallgrass of Custer State Park.

June 25, 1876, Battle of the Little Bighorn, where Custer was killed and his Seventh Cavalry was overwhelmingly defeated.

American history is everywhere in the Black Hills. A spur trail within the Black Elk Wilderness leads to Mount Rushmore National Memorial. Farther south, the trail traverses 71,000-acre Custer State Park, a stunning landscape of granite spires, clear mountain streams, and abundant wildlife from pronghorn to bighorn sheep to bison.

The trail's southernmost point traverses the pine forests, prairie dog colonies, and rolling prairies of Wind Cave National Park. The real drama here is underground in Oniya Oshoka, the place where the earth "breathes inside." This massive cavern system, 150 miles of which have been mapped, is where the Lakota believe they emerged from underground and began their life on Earth.

SOUTH DAKOTA

BLACK ELK PEAK

Summiting the Highest Point in South Dakota

DISTANCE: 7 miles round-trip **LENGTH OF TRIP:** 3 to 4 hours **BEST TIME TO GO:** Spring or fall
DIFFICULTY: Moderate

The Black Hills are a must on any cross-country road-trip itinerary. A literal high point is climbing Black Elk Peak, named in honor of the revered Oglala Lakota spiritual leader who climbed the mountain at age nine and had the first of many visions directing the fate of the Lakota people.

At 7,242 feet, this jagged pinnacle is the highest point between the Rocky Mountains and the French Pyrénées. There are multiple paths to the top, but one of the most rewarding is to start at the Cathedral Spires trailhead off the Needles Highway. The first mile requires a steep hike to the base of a series of spectacular granite slabs that soar into the sky. The trail continues down, then up through the Black Elk Wilderness, finally ascending to the summit, where a stone fire lookout, built by the Civilian Conservation Corps in the 1930s, towers above the rolling hills. At the top, hikers are rewarded with panoramic views of South Dakota, Nebraska, Wyoming, and Montana.

Surrounding the abandoned lookout are colorful prayer flags and other offerings from Lakota people who pilgrimage to the summit, especially during the spring equinox to welcome the Thunder Beings, spirits who control the weather and have the power to give life and take it away. Hikers need to be respectful of the peak's spiritual significance and should leave all prayer flags and offerings in place.

OPPOSITE: It's a 3.5-mile climb to the 7,242-foot summit of Black Elk Peak.

WISCONSIN

ICE AGE NATIONAL SCENIC TRAIL

Following the Terminal Moraine

DISTANCE: 1,200 miles one-way **LENGTH OF TRIP:** 7 to 12 weeks **BEST TIME TO GO:** Year-round
DIFFICULTY: Moderate

Most thru-hikes follow a relatively straight line along a mountain range or coastline. The Ice Age National Scenic Trail is an anomaly in that it meanders all over Wisconsin, haphazardly starting in the northwest at the St. Croix River and traversing east, then dipping dramatically south to Janesville, before U-turning north again to end on Green Bay. The erratic path is the result of the trail's unique mission, which is to follow the terminal moraine of the Laurentide ice sheet, a massive frozen ocean that covered millions of square miles and was two miles thick in places before it began to retreat 10,000 years ago.

What's the fun in tracing the end point of an ancient mass of ice? For lovers of geology, this trail is a living laboratory, offering a real-time, up-close look at erratic boulders and other forms the glacier left behind. Once you begin to understand how these features formed as the result of the retreating glacier, the landscape comes alive. What might appear to be an odd-shaped little hill is a kame, or a pile of sand, gravel, and till that accumulated in a depression of the retreating glacier. The myriad bodies of water scattered across the landscape are kettle lakes, formed when ice became buried in sediment and melted, creating a water-filled depression.

HISTORICAL FOOTNOTE

In March 2021, Emily Ford became the first woman and the second person on record to complete the Ice Age National Scenic Trail in winter. Ford completed this feat with her companion, a sled dog named Diggins. She moved on to pursue a dogsled racing career in Alaska and finished the 2025 Iditarod.

OPPOSITE: Find stacked boulders and formations at Devil's Lake State Park.

PAGES 382-383: Fall brings new perspective—and colors—to the Ice Age National Scenic Trail.

At points along the way, especially at the National Park Service's Cross Plains Interpretive Site near the southernmost tip of the trail, hikers can almost straddle an imaginary line between the glaciated landscape to the north and the Driftless Area, the region that the glacier never reached, to the south.

Beyond the geology lesson, the trail is varied and beautiful, from hardwood forests in the north to stunning prairies riddled with a rainbow of wildflowers in the south. The trail follows a corridor of hardwood and cedar forests along the Plover River, a Class I trout stream with a naturally sustaining trout population. To ensure dry feet, an all-volunteer contingent from the Ice Age Alliance laid down more than 300 stepping stones and a 1,000-foot-long boardwalk. At Devil's Lake State Park in the south—the only portion of the trail that was covered by glaciers 14,000 years ago—the path climbs dramatically up a steep series of stone steps to the top of 500-foot quartzite bluffs with views to the shimmering waters of the 360-acre lake below.

BY THE NUMBERS

- **1.8 billion years:** Age of rock outcrops at Grandfather Falls and Eau Claire Dells
- **410 to 440 million years:** Age of dolomite of the Niagara Escarpment
- **10,000 to 25,000 years:** Age of the recent glacially deposited soil, gravel, and boulders found in areas of almost every county along the trail

ABOVE: **Young hikers use a map to find where they are on the Ice Age National Scenic Trail.**

OPPOSITE: **A rolling stream makes its way through the forest at Devil's Lake State Park near Baraboo.**

Near the trail's northeastern terminus, it follows sandy Point Beach with views of vast Lake Michigan.

This rich landscape has produced some of the nation's greatest conservationists. North of Madison, the trail winds through the prairies, meadows, lakes, and woodlands that were the boyhood playground of John Muir, the founder of the Sierra Club and a founding father of the modern national park system. The trail also passes near the Aldo Leopold Legacy Center, in Baraboo, home of the famous Leopold farm and "shack," which is now a national historic landmark. In the 1930s, Leopold bought this farm and renovated the chicken coop into a simple cabin from which he could practice his environmental philosophies. Much of Leopold's writings on conservation, the environment, and wildlife, including his 1948 classic, *A Sand County Almanac,* were composed here in this quiet, unassuming enclave in Wisconsin.

WISCONSIN

SANDSPIT TRAIL

Hiking the Outer Limits in Apostle Islands National Lakeshore

DISTANCE: 7.5 miles one-way **LENGTH OF TRIP:** 4 to 6 hours **BEST TIME TO GO:** July to September
DIFFICULTY: Strenuous

The beauty and challenge of hiking in Apostle Islands National Lakeshore is that all but one of the lakeshore's 14 trails require a boat or kayak to reach. Barring that logistical puzzle, this archipelago of 22 islands, 21 of which make up the national lakeshore, is a fascinating arena of discovery within Lake Superior, the world's largest freshwater lake by surface area.

The spiritual and cultural homeland of the Ojibwe people, the islands are collectively known as Wenabozho ominisan ("Wenabozho's islands"), after the demigod who created them. Eighty percent of the islands are now federally protected wilderness, home to black bears, roughed grouse, snowshoe hares, and many species of birds including loons and the state-endangered piping plover, which nests on remote gravely beaches.

Before their natural rewilding, these islands witnessed multiple eras of human history, from the Anishinaabe people (including the Ojibwe), who fished, hunted, and gathered blueberries thousands of years ago, to timber companies that used a crew of "flying lumberjacks" in the 1950s, shuttling them from the mainland via small planes to fell hemlock forests. Scattered across the islands are seven historic light stations, most of which were built in the 1800s to aid increasing ship traffic.

One of the most fascinating hikes is on the third largest island, known as

OPPOSITE: **Wander the shore of Lake Superior.**

PAGES 388-389: **Enjoy a campfire and an overnight on Outer Island.**

Outer because it sits 25 miles off the mainland. To access its Sandspit Trail requires a well-planned kayaking voyage, private boat, or charter, which just serves to enhance this wild adventure that should be undertaken only by experienced and well-prepared hikers and paddlers. Because of its isolation and Lake Superior's treacherous and fickle weather—the year-round average water temperature is 42°F—there's a limited time window to access the trail.

It's worth a try, though. On the north end, the trail starts at the Outer Island Lighthouse, which was built in 1874 high on a cliff. Its powerful Fresnel lens projected a beam of light that was visible for 20 miles. Heading south, most of the trail forges through balsam, hemlock, yellow birch, and sugar maple forest. It can be rough in places, with dense overgrowth, because regular maintenance is nearly impossible to coordinate this far out. On the trail's south end, an enormous sandspit curls like a comma into Lake Superior. At its base is the island's sole campsite. Stay a while to explore the steep clay cliffs along the shoreline via kayak and soak in the haunting presence of human history.

HISTORICAL FOOTNOTE

A 1.5-mile spur trail near the lighthouse leads to the remains of Lullabye Lumber Camp, a former fly-in logging operation from the 1950s owned by a furniture company that manufactured baby cribs. Scattered throughout the regrown forest are cars, log cabins, cooking oil, beer bottles, and other relics of the one-time residents.

COAST TO COAST

AMERICAN DISCOVERY TRAIL

From Sea to Shining Sea

DISTANCE: 6,800 miles one-way **LENGTH OF TRIP:** 13 to 18 months **BEST TIME TO GO:** Year-round
DIFFICULTY: Strenuous

For hikers curious to discover how this vast, diverse country is stitched together step by step, here's an important number to consider: 2.6 billion. That's roughly the average number of steps it will take to complete the American Discovery Trail, which stretches from Delaware's Cape Henlopen State Park to California's Point Reyes National Seashore.

In 2005, Marcia and Ken Powers were the first people to thru-hike the trail in one continuous push from east to west, averaging more than 20 miles a day, and taking only four days off during their extraordinary 231-day trek. A more reasonable pace, however, would be to hike 15 miles a day and rest one day per week. That would take slightly more than one year, about 390 days, to cover 5,000 miles.

Like the country it traverses, the trail is a melting pot of cultures and experiences. It offers an intimate portrait of almost every American landscape, from small towns to major cities, from wide-open deserts to sheltering forests, and from dense coastal populations to the rural spaces in between.

A total of 6,800 miles, the multiuse trail connects five national scenic trails, 12 national historic trails, and 34 national recreational trails, and it passes through 14 national parks, 16 national forests, and more than 10,000 sites of historical, cultural, and natural significance. A third of the trail is singletrack;

OPPOSITE: Look out over Harpers Ferry, West Virginia, from the top of Maryland Heights.

PAGES 392-393: The American Discovery Trail connects with the Pacific Crest Trail and affords views of Donner Lake in Truckee, California.

the rest is asphalt, crushed stone, double-track, greenway, park, dirt road, or a rail-trail conversion—so hikers may also encounter cyclists or horseback riders.

Near Cincinnati, the trail splits in two, diverging north through Chicago or south through St. Louis, reconnecting again in Denver. Those who choose the northern route will shave off 200 miles, replenish calories with deep-dish pizza in Chicago, and also likely experience cooler weather. Those who choose the southern route may have a few extra blisters due to the added miles, but the payoff is warmer climes and more jazz and barbecue in Kansas City and St. Louis.

The trail reaches a height of 13,207 feet while crossing the Continental Divide over the Rocky Mountains at Argentine Pass in Colorado's Front Range. But most veteran hikers consider the toughest stretches of the American Discovery Trail to be those that cross the monotonous, rolling plains of Kansas or the parched deserts of western Utah and Nevada. These massive empty American spaces feel as if they will roll on forever.

HISTORICAL FOOTNOTE

On February 10, 2024, Briana "Rocky Mountain High" DeSanctis crossed the imaginary finish line at Point Reyes National Seashore to become the first woman to solo thru-hike the entire 6,800-mile American Discovery Trail. She relied on wilderness solitude and the kindness of friends and strangers, and wore through 27 pairs of shoes in the process.

HIKES BY LOCATION

***Bolded trails indicate multi-state routes; only beginning and terminus listed here.**

ACKNOWLEDGMENTS

I finished the first draft of this book in early 2025 amid massive layoffs across the National Park Service and other federal agencies, which sparked public outcry over the future of our public lands. I have immense gratitude for the public servants who are stewarding these trails during a fraught moment in our nation's history.

Many of these trails exist thanks to help from nonprofit partner organizations and volunteers. Dozens of people I met while researching this book have spent countless hours fundraising, advocating for, or maintaining their beloved backyard trail simply to provide a path that will bring joy to fellow hikers. Thank you for your work that never ends.

I have hiked many, but not all, of the trails I chose for this book. I'm grateful to those who generously shared their time and knowledge, especially about trails I have yet to complete.

This book is a beauty. Credit for its excellence goes to the talented team at National Geographic. Thank you, editor Allyson Johnson, for being a thoughtful, kind, positive force behind the project. A heartfelt thanks to designer Kay Hankins, photo editor Uliana Bazar, senior photo editor and rights manager Meredith Wilcox, senior production editor Michael O'Connor, senior production manager Anne LeongSon, and creative director Elisa Gibson for your roles in creating this elegant book. A shout-out to Kate Siber, author of National Geographic's *100 Hikes of a Lifetime* international version for her guidance and friendship.

My late parents, David and Judy Pearson, taught me by example that hiking is the simplest path to joy and freedom. They logged thousands of miles over decades in Sedona, Arizona, instilling in friends and family countless moments of trail magic. My partner Brian gamely hiked through thunderstorms and up mountain summits and drove cross-country to help me research this book. His patience, levity, and kindness kept us going. To all family and friends with whom I've shared a trail, I am grateful for every one of you and hope our paths continue to merge in the years to come.

ABOUT THE AUTHOR

Stephanie Pearson is a 2023 National Geographic Explorer and a former editor at *Outside* magazine. She is the author of National Geographic's *100 Great American Parks* and a children's book, *50 True Tales From Our Great National Parks.*

Pearson earned a master's degree from Northwestern University's Medill School of Journalism, then began her career at *Outside*, where she was on the editorial staff for 13 years. Her freelance assignments have included reporting from Mount Everest Base Camp, meditating with Tibetan Buddhist scholar Robert Thurman in Bhutan, and writing an online science curriculum for elementary students while traveling through Latin America and Australia with fellow National Geographic Explorer Dan Buettner.

Pearson has been honored to receive several Lowell Thomas Awards from the Society of American Travel Writers, including the 2023 Gold Award for Travel Journalist of the Year. Lately she's become preoccupied with exploring the lakes and trails in her own northern Minnesota backyard.

Find her on Instagram *(@stephanieapearson)*, at the National Geographic Explorer Home Page, or on her website, *stephanieannpearson.com.*

ILLUSTRATIONS CREDITS

Cover, Grant Ordelheide/TandemStock; back cover, skiserge1/iStock/Getty Images; 2-3, Dan Holz/TandemStock; 4-5, Thomas Barwick/DigitalVision/Getty Images; 7, Paul Williams/NPL/Minden Pictures; 8-9, Sean Pavone/Alamy Stock Photo; 10, Michael Jones/Design Pics/Alamy Stock Photo; 12-3, Roman Khomlyak/iStock/Getty Images; 15, Walter Meayers Edwards/National Geographic Image Collection; 16-7, Matt Propert; 18, Pete McBride/National Geographic Image Collection; 19, Michael Nolan/robertharding; 21, Whit Richardson/Cavan Images; 22-3, Ian Shive/TandemStock; 25, Kyle George/Cavan Images/Alamy Stock Photo; 26-7, Ron Niebrugge/Alamy Stock Photo; 29, Ronda Brady/Shutterstock; 31, Michael Okimoto/Cavan Images; 33, Blake Burton/Cavan Images/Alamy Stock Photo; 35, yhelfman/iStock/Getty Images; 37, HagePhoto/Cavan Images/Alamy Stock Photo; 38-9, Hans Harms/iStock/Getty Images; 41, Ryan Heffernan/Cavan Images/Alamy Stock Photo; 42-3, PictureLake/E+/Getty Images; 44, Dave Fleishman—Just a Little Light Fine Photography/iStock/Getty Images; 45, Ryan Heffernan/Cavan Images/Alamy Stock Photo; 47, Michael DeYoung Photography/TandemStock; 48-9, Jeff Lewis (landESCAPEvisuals)/TandemStock; 50, Clark Ahlstrom/iStock/Getty Images; 51, Brown W. Cannon III/Cavan Images/Alamy Stock Photo; 53, Chris Swartwood/Cavan Images; 55, Pavel Chigir/Shutterstock; 56-7, Craig Zerbe/iStock/Getty Images; 58, Colin D. Young/Shutterstock; 59, Kennan Harvey; 61, Scott Hardesty/Cavan Images; 63, Mark Lisk/Alamy Stock Photo; 65, Jason Savage/TandemStock; 67, Sean Jansen/iStock/Getty Images; 68-9, Colton Stiffler; 70, Andy Austin; 71, Jess McGlothlin Media/Cavan Images; 73, Lifestyle/Alamy Stock Photo; 75, Ethan Welty/Alamy Stock Photo; 76-7, NPS Photo; 78, Ian Shive/TandemStock; 79, Rich Reid/TandemStock; 81, Kennan Harvey/Cavan Images; 82-3, Emily Polar/TandemStock; 84, Austin Trigg/TandemStock; 85, Andrew R. Slaton/TandemStock; 87, Chris Moore—Exploring Light Photography/TandemStock; 89, Tim Fitzharris/Minden Pictures; 90-1, halbergman/E+/Getty Images; 92, Justin Bailie/TandemStock; 93, Tom Schwabel/TandemStock; 95, Larry Geddis/Alamy Stock Photo; 97, NPS Photo/Alamy Stock Photo; 99, Valentin Wolf/imageBROKER/Getty Images; 100-1, Frank Bach/Shutterstock; 102, Allen.G/Adobe Stock; 103, Bartfett/iStock/Getty Images; 105, Frans Lanting/National Geographic Image Collection; 107, Suzanne Stroeer/Cavan Images/Alamy Stock Photo; 108-9, Barrett Hedges/National Geographic Image Collection; 110, Pete McBride/National Geographic Image Collection; 111, Suzanne Stroeer/Cavan Images/Alamy Stock Photo; 113, Spring Images/Alamy Stock Photo; 114-5, Gary Luhm/DanitaDelimont/Alamy Stock Photo; 116, Larry Geddis/Alamy Stock Photo; 117, Kelly vanDellen/Alamy Stock Photo; 119, Forest2Sea/Adobe Stock; 120-1, Chad Ehlers/Alamy Stock Photo; 123, Austin Cronnelly/TandemStock; 124-5, skiserge1/iStock/Getty Images; 127, Ben Herndon/TandemStock; 128-9, Don White/iStock/Getty Images; 131, HagePhoto/Cavan Images; 133, Michael Jones/Design Pics/Alamy Stock Photo; 134-5, Ron Niebrugge/Alamy Stock Photo; 137, Floris van Breugel/Nature Picture Library/Alamy Stock Photo; 138-9, David Moskowitz/TandemStock; 140, Michael Melford/Design Pics/Alamy Stock Photo; 141, Jonathan Irish/National Geographic Image Collection; 143, Morgan Trimble/Alamy Stock Photo; 145, Pep Roig/Alamy Stock Photo; 146-7, Eric Kolb/Alamy Stock Photo; 148, Jason Pineau/All Canada Photos/Alamy Stock Photo; 149, Pep Roig/Alamy Stock Photo; 151, NPS Photo; 152-3, Brenda Smith DVM/Shutterstock; 155, Janelle Orth/Alamy Stock Photo; 156-7, Ryan Ecal/Shutterstock; 159, Sergio Ballivian/TandemStock; 160-1, Ron Niebrugge/Alamy Stock Photo; 162, Billy McDonald/Alamy Stock Photo; 163, Janine/Adobe Stock; 165, Alex Messenger/TandemStock; 166-7, Goss Images/Alamy Stock Photo; 169, Michael DeFreitas North America/Alamy Stock Photo; 171, Alex Ship/Shutterstock; 173, Bebi Church; 174-5, Emanuel Ortiz Rolón/Alamy Stock Photo; 177, Alison Langley/Cavan Images; 178-9, Kerrick James/Alamy Stock Photo; 180, Leon Werdinger/Alamy Stock Photo; 181, bluepompano/

iStock/Getty Images; 182–3, Larry Gloth/Moment/Getty Images; 185, Jerry and Marcy Monkman/EcoPhotography/Alamy Stock Photo; 187, Bill Crnkovich/Alamy Stock Photo; 188–9, Yvonne Navalaney/Shutterstock; 191, Kennan Harvey/Cavan Images/Alamy Stock Photo; 192–3, Pete Muller/National Geographic Image Collection; 194, Jon Bilous/Alamy Stock Photo; 195, Cavan Images/Chris Bennett/Getty Images; 197, Chris Bennett/Cavan Images; 198–9, Design Pics/Natural Selection Robert Cable/Getty Images; 200, Scott Suriano/Moment/Getty Images; 201, Jerry Monkman/Cavan Images; 203–5, Norman Eggert/Alamy Stock Photo; 207, Jay Yuan/Shutterstock; 209, Littleny/Alamy Stock Photo; 210–1, George Ostertag/Alamy Stock Photo; 213, Brent Doscher/Cavan Images/Alamy Stock Photo; 214–5, Vlad G/Shutterstock; 217, Daniel Westergren/National Geographic Image Collection; 218–9, Jose Azel/National Geographic Image Collection; 221, Leembe/iStock/Getty Images; 222–3, Gabby Salazar/National Geographic Image Collection; 225, Francis/Adobe Stock; 227, Nature's Charm/Shutterstock; 228–9, Chris Murray/Cavan Images; 231, H. Mark Weidman Photography/Alamy Stock Photo; 232–3, Walt Bilous/Alamy Stock Photo; 235, Cavan Images/Cate Brown/Shutterstock; 236–7, Cate Brown/Cavan Images; 239, Corey Hendrickson/Cavan Images; 240–1, John Lazenby/Alamy Stock Photo; 242, Kurt Budliger/TandemStock; 243, Alexander Nesbitt/Cavan Images; 245, Daniel Holz/TandemStock; 247, Jon Bilous/Shutterstock; 249, Wayne Wolfersberger/Shutterstock; 251, Bkamprath/E+/Getty Images; 252–3, Tim Pennington/iStock/Getty Images; 254–5, Carlton Ward Jr.; 257, Stephen Alvarez/National Geographic Image Collection; 258–9, Christopher Krato/Dreamstime; 261, korkeakoski/Adobe Stock; 263, T. C. Knight/Design Pics/Alamy Stock Photo; 265–7, Peter Essick/Cavan Images/Alamy Stock Photo; 269, Andrew R. Slaton/TandemStock; 270–1, Mac Stone/TandemStock; 273, Colin D. Young/Alamy Stock Photo; 274–5, Made For More Productions/Shutterstock; 277, Ken Martin/Alamy Stock Photo; 279, Robert Loe/Moment/Getty Images; 281, Sandra Burm/Alamy Stock Photo; 282–3, Chris Dixon/The New York Times/Redux; 285, Itziar Aio/Moment/Getty Images; 286–7, Mike Wilkinson/Alamy Stock Photo; 289, Mario Villafuerte/The New York Times/Redux; 290–1, Jonathan Nutt/Moment/Getty Images; 293, Steven Reich/iStock/Getty Images; 295, Pavo Real /Alamy Stock Photo; 297, Pat & Chuck Blackley/Alamy Stock Photo; 298–9, Chansak Joe/iStock/Getty Images; 300, J Paulson/Shutterstock; 301, Bill Gozansky/Alamy Stock Photo; 303, Doug Priebe/Alamy Stock Photo; 304–5, Sari ONeal/Shutterstock; 307, Castle Light Images/Alamy Stock Photo; 309, JNix/Shutterstock; 310–1, Pat & Chuck Blackley/Alamy Stock Photo; 313, Billy McDonald/Adobe Stock; 314–5, John D. Simmons/Charlotte Observer/Tribune News Service via Getty Images; 316, Jason Childs/500px/Getty Images; 317, Susan Ruggles/Photodisc/Getty Images; 319, Tim Fitzharris/Minden Pictures; 320–1, Andrew R. Slaton/TandemStock; 322, Kelly vanDellen/Alamy Stock Photo; 323, Karl Schatz/Cavan Images/Alamy Stock Photo; 325, Billy McDonald/Adobe Stock; 326–7, zrfphoto/iStock/Getty Images; 329, Bill Gozansky/Alamy Stock Photo; 331, Tim Fitzharris/Minden Pictures; 333–5, Clint Farlinger/Alamy Stock Photo; 337, Morgan Heim/TandemStock; 339, Alex Messenger/TandemStock; 340–1, Jim Brandenburg/Minden Pictures; 342, Aaron Black-Schmidt/TandemStock; 343, Stephanie Vermillion; 345, Brandon Flint/TandemStock; 347, wildnerdpix/Alamy Stock Photo; 349, Alex Messenger/TandemStock; 350–1, James Schwabel/Alamy Stock Photo; 352, Peter Elvin/Alamy Stock Photo; 353, Jeffrey Phelps/Cavan Images/Alamy Stock Photo; 355, Tom Uhlman/Alamy Stock Photo; 356–7, Bill Grant/Alamy Stock Photo; 359, Lex Nast/Shutterstock; 361, Chuck Haney/DanitaDelimont/Alamy Stock Photo; 362–4, Michael Melford/National Geographic Image Collection; 365, Andre Jenny/Alamy Stock Photo; 367, Tim Fitzharris/Minden Pictures; 368–9, Mike Wilkinson; 371, Stephanie Vermillion; 373, Gunther Fraulob/iStock/Getty Images; 374–5, Craig Zerbe/Adobe Stock; 376, Cheri Alguire/Cavan Images; 377, Dennis Laughlin/Shutterstock; 379, Trica J. Photos/Alamy Stock Photo; 381, Kris Wiktor/Alamy Stock Photo; 382–3, Jeffrey Phelps/Cavan Images; 384, Maryna Gumenyuk/Alamy Stock Photo; 385, Jeffrey Phelps/Cavan Images; 387, Thomas Lazar/NPL/Minden Pictures; 388–9, David Guttenfelder/National Geographic Image Collection; 391, Jon Bilous/Shutterstock; 392–3, Paul Hamill/TandemStock.

Since 1888, the National Geographic Society has funded more than 15,000 research, conservation, education, technology, and storytelling projects around the world. National Geographic Partners distributes a portion of the funds it receives from your purchase to National Geographic Society to support their mission to illuminate and protect the wonder of our world.

National Geographic Partners, LLC
1145 17th Street NW
Washington, DC 20036-4688 USA

Get closer to National Geographic Explorers and photographers, and connect with our global community. Join us today at nationalgeographic.org/joinus

For rights or permissions inquiries, please contact National Geographic Books Subsidiary Rights: bookrights@natgeo.com

ISBN: 978-1-4262-2486-7

The authorized representative in the EU for product safety and compliance is Disney Trading B.V., Asterweg 15S, 1031 HL, Amsterdam, The Netherlands
email: DCP.DL-EU.bookscontact@disney.com

Printed in South Korea

26/QPSK/1